NETWORKING

▪▪▪▪ *for* ▪▪▪▪

WRITERS

WORKBOOK

PRACTICAL STRATEGIES
for NETWORKING SUCCESS

LINDA RUGGERI

To every writer who knows in their heart this is the work they were meant to do.

CONTENTS

FOREWORD

When I gave my keynote speech at the Editorial Freelancers Association Conference in 2023, I had no idea I would be invited to write this foreword. I had not yet met Linda Ruggeri, but like many fortuitous things that happen when you are open to meeting new people and getting to know them, we would soon become acquainted through a mutual friend. (That friend, Cody Sisco, and I met under nearly identical circumstances: I happened to be giving a speech at an event he was attending, and we connected.) I use the phrase "meeting new people and getting to know them" because it is not intimidating to say that. The truth, though, is that these words can easily be summed up in a single word: networking.

Linda Ruggeri has done the yeoman's work of removing all of the fear and dread that many associate with that word and replacing it with easily digestible information and actionable items that any writer can do to build strong relationships. *Networking for Writers* is the book I wish had existed when I first began my career. It breaks down the various elements of building relationships with others—and not in a superficial, self-serving way either. This workbook will help you to build the kinds of bonds that will hopefully endure throughout your career and life.

The beautiful thing about networking is that each day provides a new opportunity to build new relationships. I plan to use this book as a way of making the most of the relationships I have yet to build, and I hope once you've had a chance to explore this book that you will do the same.

RAN WALKER

INTRODUCTION

In her book *Making a Literary Life*, author Carolyn See talks about how, when she was an associate professor of English at Loyola Marymount University, the parents of one of her students wanted to meet with her because they were so worried about their nineteen-year-old son, Herbert. Carolyn tells them they have nothing to worry about, that Herbert's pulling straight As in all his classes with her, that he's wonderful, and she asks them what they're afraid about. The mom replies, "We're afraid he wants to be a writer."

I wrote my first novella when I was thirteen and living in Córdoba, Argentina. I like to think it was also my first incursion into self-publishing: I had a complete storyline with two characters; I knew my genre and target audience; I keyed it on my typewriter, drew the book cover, hand-stitched the binding of all twelve pages, and gave it to a friend for her birthday. Done, published. In turn, she passed it on to the other friends in our group, and suddenly I had a little fan community of six readers.

My writing portfolio expanded when I added humorous rhyming poems (that were simply terrible), long newsletter-like missives to classmates who were ill and had to miss school, and multiple-page love letters when I discovered boys in my late teens. My project on *La Florida del Inca*—based on the book by Inca Garcilaso de la Vega—was one of many essays and monographs in high school that kept me engaged and entertained for hours. Then two years of *periodismo* (journalism) and a degree in communications and fine arts (plus constant reading) rounded up my education with "words."

That was my calling: reading and writing. Observing and telling stories. It's all I wanted to do. Even when my dad insisted I should become an astronaut.

It took me years to believe I could make it as a writer, so instead, I became a nonfiction editor. That paid the bills and taught me how to work for and with traditional publishing houses, indie publishers, and self-published authors. It was a hands-on education of the publishing world, teaching me who needed to be on my radar if I ever wanted to make it in this industry in a non-traditional way.

The writing, editing, and publishing work I'd done for others over the years allowed me to surround myself with knowledgeable people who could teach me, who I could work with, and above all, who I could count on.

In 2021 I coauthored and also self-published *Networking for Freelance Editors*, which led to presentations, speaking invitations, panels, courses and an Independent Book Publishers Association (IBPA) Benjamin Franklin Award silver medal. And... it also led me to write this book! Because I too, as a writer and a published author, struggled with networking. And what I've learned, and what's worked for me, is in this book. The resources, examples, and real-life perspectives in this book come from my experiences and the experiences of other successful published writers I've met along the way.

WHO THIS BOOK IS FOR

Networking for Writers is the guide for you if you're looking to create, strengthen, or revamp your current network—whether that's because it's not a supportive community, you haven't found your community yet, or the hoped-for income, sales, and opportunities haven't shown up the way you expected them to. And a weak, disjointed network is most likely the cause of that. It's also a book for those looking to create a publishing team they can work with and rely on now and in the future.

As an editor turned author, networking has helped me during my writing journey to not only build an audience, but to get my book into the hands of its intended readers and receive the positive reviews it has. Many of the concepts in this book are similar to my previous book, *Networking for Freelance Editors*, but the content has been updated for the unique writer experience, and the resources, examples, and real-life perspectives come from the experience of other successful published writers I've met along the way.

What I've learned by attending writing and publishing conferences is that there seems to be this idea that networking and creatives don't go together. As if people who network are only *business people*, and people who write can only be *creative people*. But the reality is that we can and should be both: creative entrepreneurs. We have stories to tell, readers to educate, entertain or inspire. We want to be published, sell our work, and pay our bills. Each of those things doesn't exclude the others.

Every successful published writer (traditional, indie, or self) will tell you that once you publish something (a screenplay, an article, a book), you become a *business owner*, whether you had intended to or not. You have a product to sell, and as the creator of that product, you are now the owner. As a new business owner, you need to make sure your "company" is set up correctly and you're doing what you need to do so your creation reaches its intended audience.

If you're a well-established writer, chances are that you've built a publishing network that's meeting your basic needs, and that's good! But I want to help you go beyond that and turn your network into something rich and dynamic—with resources, opportunities, and strong and meaningful contacts that will help you boost your exposure, credibility, and sales.

I wrote this book to help you create a networking practice that works for you—one that incorporates your goals, your communication style, the activities you enjoy, and the tools and resources that are available to you today. Though networking may seem like an overwhelming task, you'll soon discover that building the network you need is completely within your power, with the time and space available to you now. That network will be uniquely yours because it will be built on your goals, your strengths, and your everyday activities.

In my experience as a published indie author, effective networking is all-encompassing—it's about making *connections*. Note that I won't be making a distinction between networking with other authors and networking with potential readers, organizations, clients, or publishers. Yes, there is a difference, but to a large extent, your different audiences will overlap—and they will each have access to the "you" you put out into the world.

To network effectively today, we need to be *prepared* to network. And that's what much of this book is about: taking an integrated, whole-business approach to creating relationships and opportunities. To do this, you'll find practical steps with a mindset that asks, *How can I contribute?* The practical steps identify *where* to network, and the generous mindset, unique to you as a writer, shows you *how* to interact once you're there.

In my own experience, effective networking is based on authentic relationships. And to build relationships, you have to be ready to give—of yourself, your wisdom, your empathy, your enthusiasm, your experience. Your greatest asset is that you have something the members of your network need—you. And by putting yourself in spaces where you can interact with them, whether virtually or in real life, you give yourself the opportunity to get to know and help others... and to be known and helped as well.

HOW TO USE THIS WORKBOOK

Networking for Writers is based on an interactive, step-by-step approach intended for *all* writers, whether you're a writer of novels, a freelance writer or ghostwriter, or a writer of medical or science papers. If you write plays, screenplays, sitcoms, songs, short stories, poetry, articles, novels, or prescriptive nonfiction, this book is for you. If you write memoirs, speeches, web copy, or fiction of any kind, this book is also for you.

When should you use this book? The moment you have a writing project in mind. Don't wait until you complete your manuscript to approach the subject of networking. Dedicate a few minutes every day to reading and working on some of the exercises in this book. I like to read and work on them first thing in the morning for about twenty minutes with my first cup of coffee. But you may prefer to tackle the subject late at night, after you've completed your writing goal of the day. It doesn't matter when you use it, but that you do a little bit every day.

There are two kinds of worksheets that I'll share with you throughout this book: self-assessment worksheets, which will reveal bite-size pieces of information you need to know about yourself, and the Quarterly Networking Worksheet, which will help you set goals and implement your networking plan in a manageable way.

If you have the e-book version of the book, I recommend printing the worksheets out and working through them as drafts before settling on your final networking plan. These worksheets can be downloaded from www.networkingforeditors.com/resources.

The steps that we'll cover in the following chapters include

- Understanding what networking is and why it's valuable

- Evaluating your current network and identifying opportunities for growth

- Determining your networking goals and who you need to reach

- Exploring five networking tactics
    - A website
    - Personal communications
    - Social media
    - Professional groups
    - Volunteering

- Discovering your personal networking style

As diverse as our writing niches or genres may be, our core networking goals are the same: to be part of a supportive community and to connect with readers we can entertain, inspire, help, or inform.

As with everything in life, there are no magic results without putting in the work that's needed. In the words of author Susan Cain in her book *Quiet: The Power of Introverts in a World That Can't Stop Talking*, "Take what applies to you, and use the rest to improve your relationships with others."

GETTING TO KNOW EACH OTHER

Before we start connecting with others, we need to know *how to describe ourselves* and *how to frame what we do*. Let me tell you a bit about myself; then you can share your introduction using the following guide.

Me

My name is Linda Ruggeri, and I'm a bilingual nonfiction writer and editor based out of Los Angeles. I specialize in writing and editing prescriptive nonfiction and the review of Spanish translations of books for all age groups.

You

Now, practice introducing yourself using the same format, or something like it, in the blank space beneath the bullet points below. Get the most important information about who you are into two or three lines you can easily remember, but that also tell people exactly what type of writer you are. Don't forget to include

- your full name or pen name, or both,
- if you are a fiction or nonfiction writer,
- your genre/area of expertise/passion,
- the age group you write for, i.e., early-level readers, middle grade (MG), young adult (YA), teen, adult (if applicable), and
- your home city.

Your introduction

_____

_____

_____

_____

_____

_____

To have a successful experience with this book, let's establish what you are hoping to get from it and from the work you'll be doing. My goals in reading this book are

_____

_____

_____

_____

_____

_____

Now I can say, "Nice to meet you!"

I look forward to going on this networking journey together!

I'M READY TO GROW MY NETWORK,

HELP OTHERS, AND LEVEL UP MY BUSINESS.

PART 1

REIMAGINING NETWORKING

We've all been networking most our lives with varying degrees of success. What's going to change today is *how* you think of networking. Together, we are going to reimagine networking into something that truly benefits who you are as a writer.

CHAPTER 1

NETWORKING NOW

> *Networking is everywhere. Successful networking requires understanding the immense power of regular daily activities to connect with someone else.*
>
> —*J. KELLY HOEY*, BUILD YOUR DREAM NETWORK

Let's be frank. Many of us come to networking with a sense of dread. We think of it as transactional and potentially awkward. Though we've been told for years that networking is critical to our success, so much of what we know about it comes from the traditional business world, with its cleanly delineated, compartmentalized organizational charts and clear career paths. Meanwhile, as writers, we're in a "Create Your Own Career" environment. Our needs are different. Our challenges are many. And we often lack access to the supportive infrastructure of a "regular" workplace with its camaraderie, opportunities for mentorship, and built-in training and recognition processes.

When we're sitting (or standing) at our desks, trying to find the ideal readers (or clients), productive networking may seem like something that's beyond our reach. But what I've discovered is that as writers we're in a unique position to network in an integrated, personalized way—one that's suited to the realities of our online and offline world. We just have to shift our perspective and make intentional use of the tools available to us.

WHAT IS NETWORKING?

At its core, **networking is behavior that builds a web of mutually beneficial relationships**. Like most relationships, our network is built over time, through everyday interactions—like being reliable, listening, keeping others' needs in mind, and reaching out to show support or give encouragement. These small actions reveal character, build connections, and create a space for us to get to know one another. And as our relationships grow, we find ourselves in an interlaced community that supports us and gives us opportunities to support others.

What activities "count" as networking? Let's apply our definition of networking to various activities and consider how they measure up.

Networking is...

- offering insights or sharing knowledge with kindness and tact,
- helping clients or vendors connect with others if you aren't able to help them,
- maintaining long-term contact with colleagues, clients, service providers, or vendors,
- answering questions from new authors, writers, or readers,
- sending colleagues links related to their writing niches when we come across them,
- sharing contest or event information with fellow authors,
- collaborating or cross-promoting to gain a wider readership, and
- sharing resources, relevant news, or job opportunities with fellow writers.

In other words, networking is building long-lasting professional relationships by sharing resources, expertise, and support.

Networking isn't...

- exchanging business cards, then dumping them in a drawer;
- ranting on forums;
- offering **unsolicited** corrections or writing advice;
- using your knowledge to put others down;
- asking others for their email list or agent's number;
- collecting random LinkedIn connections;
- expecting direct, tangible repayment for help you provide or referrals you make; or
- "emoji commenting," i.e., wholesale "liking" posts without commenting and engaging.

In other words, networking isn't transactional, impersonal, self-aggrandizing, or aimless.

If your idea of networking lines up with the first list, then you're off to a great start. But if the activities in the "Networking isn't" list look like the kind of networking you're familiar with, don't fret. Networking isn't something we learned in school. It can vary widely by culture, location, and industry. So, let's take this opportunity to reframe our thoughts around networking and explore how to network within the freelance or indie writing field.

I'll add my only disclaimer here: my networking approach focuses on the positive and on giving back. Why? Because in my experience this is the type of networking that has the best results—both in terms of tangible success (often measured in reader, vendor, and client relationships) and in developing a professional support system. Networking not only grows our business, establishes lifelong working relationships, and increases our income, but it can also provide us with emotional support and give us opportunities to socialize with like-minded people.

NETWORKING BEHAVIORS

Networking opportunities come in many forms, and while it's possible for some behaviors to fall squarely under "not networking," it's also possible for one activity to be either "networking" or "not networking" depending on whether we *engage* in it with a networking mindset and intentionality—or we just do it on autopilot.

Remember to use the definition "behavior that builds a web of mutually beneficial relationships" to test whether activities are worth investing in as part of a networking strategy. We find that framing this as a simple question keeps us mindful of our purpose so we don't get overwhelmed or offtrack.

Next up is a basic networking mind map, or visual diagram, with some everyday activities. As we work through the following chapters, we'll explore these activities and how they serve us as networking touchpoints. For now, review this sample mind map and ask of each example activity, *How can this behavior help me build a web of mutually beneficial relationships?* If the connection isn't clear yet, that's okay. We still have much to discuss!

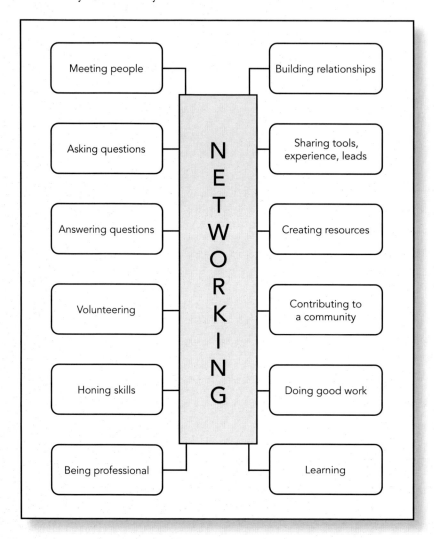

Sample networking mind map with possible networking activities.

Now use the following blank networking mind map to list activities that you think could be part of your networking plan. For each activity, ask the question, *How can this behavior help me build a web of mutually beneficial relationships?* If you don't have good answers yet, don't worry. The important thing here is to open our minds to the possibilities of what behaviors and activities can serve our networking today, as opposed to the tired old formulas of yesterday. Once you've filled in at least six spaces, set the mind map aside.

Practice networking mind map with possible networking activities.

In the following chapters, we'll explore how these (and other) activities work within a networking framework.

A WRITER'S PERSPECTIVE

Networking has helped me get my name out there. When people learn more about what I do and why, it tends to stick with them. I've often gotten referrals from people I don't even know because they remember something important about me or they recall hearing my name associated with the work that I love doing. It has meant that I'm even benefiting from networks that I didn't yet know that I was a part of!

—**EBONYE GUSSINE WILKINS,** FOUNDER OF INCLUSIVE MEDIA SOLUTIONS LLC
AND AUTHOR OF *Respectful Querying with NUANCE*

CHAPTER 2

UNDERSTANDING YOUR NETWORK

> *To get the best, you must surround yourself with the most outstanding, caring, and helpful people.*
>
> —RICK FRISHMAN AND JILL LUBLIN, NETWORKING MAGIC

Take a minute to think about how much socializing changed after Covid-19 came into the world. For many of us, in order to cope and stay afloat, we had to reach out and depend on new people—and be even more present for those close to us. We discovered new ways to work, to adjust, to relate, and to keep going. We built new networks without knowing it, reinforced other networks we had let dwindle, and treasured dearly the networks we couldn't live without.

We also came back with a different perspective on how we wanted to live our lives and on what we wanted to do (i.e., finally write that book!), and we chose to let go of networks that no longer served us.

Who are the people that you surround yourself with in your daily life (in person or virtually)? How do you relate to them? How do you support each other, and why does it matter? What are the activities you've let go of, either because you don't have the bandwidth, because you want to scale down, because you moved to a new city, or because you want to move in a different writing direction? In this chapter, we're going to examine these connections and understand how they bring value to our lives as indie authors.

In the book *Quiet*, author Susan Cain talks about a problem-solving activity called the Subarctic Survival Situation. In this exercise, participants in a group have to imagine an extreme survival situation, like an arctic plane crash, where they only get to take fifteen items off that plane with them, and they have to rank those items in order of importance. The exercise is intended to take you out of your everyday role and area of expertise and make you use your synergistic problem-solving skills to survive.

Although writing and publishing don't even come close to an arctic plane crash, sometimes it can feel like we're headed in that direction ("the Self-Publishing Survival Situation"). Take a minute to think about it. If you need to launch your writer website, or publish your book, or produce that podcast within the next six months, who are the fifteen people you'd want to have with you? And can you rank them in order of importance? Who are we really connecting with, and are we prioritizing building good relationships with those we need to have close to us to be successful?

THE TWO NETWORKS

As J. Kelly Hoey explains in *Build Your Dream Network*, there are two types of networks, and we need both to succeed.

The Small, Trusted Network

When the whole world is open to us through the internet, and when many writing conferences are accessible by virtue of being online and therefore more affordable than in-person attendance, it may feel like our potential network is... everyone on the planet. Particularly for writers who are just starting out, there's a strong desire to connect with *anyone* who might be able to help us along our career path. But no matter where we are in our journey, we all need a primary safe space where we can share our experiences, both positive and negative, and learn from them. Quite often, this supportive environment isn't found in the wilds of cyberspace.

In everyday practice, we create this safe place by building a small, trusted network. Think of it as a networking home base. This close network usually consists of a few individuals we can go to with questions and doubts. It's where we discuss work challenges, share wins, refer clients or colleagues, and offer support. The feedback we receive here really counts because it's coming from peers we trust and look up to and from mentors and colleagues who have our best interests at heart. These are the people we go to with questions that we might be uncomfortable asking in a large group—like on an international discussion list or a Facebook authors' group.

The small, trusted network is somewhere we can be vulnerable, where there's a good balance of give and take. In my experience, colleagues who are at similar places in their careers are often the best fit for this network because they are dealing with comparable issues and are invested in solving the challenges that crop up at that specific stage of the writing career. But it's also great to have a few more experienced connections in the small, trusted network because they can act as mentors and guides. In turn, as we gain experience, we act as mentors for newer colleagues. **If you're a beginner to writing as a career, work on building your close network first.**

It's in the small, close network that we have the opportunity for a deeper level of engagement and reciprocity so we can ask the hard questions or give the hard feedback (in a kind way). Our small professional network is like a group of friends (a place of trust, dependability, listening), but it will always be exclusively related to our work as writers. That said, in this network, we'll likely go beyond the usual professional-level interactions, supporting each other the same way we would take care of our friends—by checking in with them, sending them an occasional note or message, and celebrating their successes. It sounds a lot like friendship, right? But it isn't necessarily (though some people in this network may turn out to be friends too).

So, how do we build that close network?

As with networking in general, it takes time to build relationships. Places to start connecting with other writing professionals are associations like the American Medical Writers Association (AMWA), the National Association of Science Writers (NASW), the Authors Guild, Contemporary Romance Writers (CRW), the Native American Journalists Association, Freelancers Union, Mystery Writers of America (MWA), Sisters in Crime, or the American Society of Journalists and Authors (ASJA). Note, a more exhaustive list is in appendix A.

Don't be afraid to reach out to people whose posts are positive and friendly and introduce yourself. In particular, focus on people who share your writing niche or who are asking (or providing helpful answers to) the questions that are most pressing in your work. Rewarding business relationships and friendships often begin with the courage to reach out.

Another great way to connect with authors or writers who are at similar places in their careers is to take classes (in person or online) and get to know fellow students. While this is a bit harder for asynchronous classes (but can still be done), I've found that classes that have a group discussion component are excellent opportunities to expand and deepen our networks. How productive the discussion space is often depends on how well the instructor sets the tone and guides the conversation, so don't give up if one class doesn't further your networking goals. (Here I'll give a shout-out to romance writing instructor Jeanne De Vita and writing craft instructor Jordan Rosenfeld whose skills in community building make their classes great places to both learn and develop relationships.)

Once you start building trusted, two-way relationships with individual writers, you may find there's so much knowledge and support being shared that you want to start connecting members of your network with each other. (Remember, just because it's a small network doesn't mean all the members know each other; it just means you know them because they are in your network.) And here's the great thing about this approach to networking—it spreads the benefits and builds community, instead of hoarding them and reinforcing isolation. Once you reach this point in your networking journey, you may be ready to consider forming a mastermind group, which is a cooperative group of peers who come together for growth, learning, and support. If this sounds intriguing, check out the next section for more about mastermind groups and how to create your own. Another option for those who prefer a one-on-one approach is to find a colleague you have a rapport with and become accountability partners.

Mastermind Groups (A.K.A. The Business-Oriented Writing Group)

A mastermind group is a group of dependable people who share similar career objectives and work together to support each other in reaching those goals. Mastermind groups are very different from writer groups because they provide peer *business* accountability (remember how we said your book is your business in the introduction?). They also offer support, shared resources, inspiration, education, networking, and much more. The advantages of belonging to a mastermind group are many: it's a closed group; it's a safe place for developing long-lasting relationships built on trust; and it's made of colleagues you can rely on when you have questions and doubts or need help finding resources.

As an example, my mastermind group started pretty organically, and it was definitely a result of good networking! I roomed with a fellow editor at a conference (who I hadn't met in person yet) who was also interested in being in a mastermind group, and we both ended up asking other people who we knew, and voila! Here we are, more than five years later, still meeting, still working on our goals, all of us with writing projects of our own (besides the editing work we do)—and we all have stronger businesses and happier professional lives because of it.

Through this mastermind group, we've learned a lot from each other. Above all, I've gained confidence in myself. This mastermind group has taught each one of us why we are worth it and how much we can accomplish individually but also together.

There are many books and websites with suggestions for how to start a successful mastermind group, and for reference, I've listed some in appendix B.

In my experience, when setting up a writing mastermind group, it's best to

1. Keep it small. This way, each topic you're working on can be properly discussed, and each participant has time to share, as well as give feedback or ask questions.

2. Keep your meetings organized. Use a pre-established agenda for each one (so you stay on track) with an *estimated* time to spend on each item. (For agenda structure ideas, see the end of this section.)

3. Be flexible. There are no set rules—only the ones you establish as a group. Choose the meeting topics according to what works for *your* group and what everyone is interested in achieving for themselves. Change, skip, or move agendas as you all see fit depending on the group's needs. Remember, this isn't a writing group, but a group of writers who are looking to grow their writing business.

4. Set time limits. Some mastermind groups have meetings that go from one to two hours per session and meet every two or three weeks. This allows everyone enough time to follow through on the goals they are working on, or to research a discussion topic they can share with the group.

5. Remember, it's not a friendship (though it can turn into one). You don't have to be friends with or know everyone in your group when starting out. The idea is to surround yourself with writers who have different perspectives and experiences than you have, so you can learn about how others work, what works for them, what tools they use, what their experience is like, what their highs and lows are, and how they get through them. The perspective you gain from others will help you approach your own work challenges with new insights. It can also help you disengage from the stress of being wrapped up in your own head.

6. Be committed. You must commit to showing up—for the group, for the work, for yourself. It's okay if you have to miss a meeting (though often the group may choose to reschedule it), but make this group time a priority. Remember, it's time away from work that has the potential to produce income for you, so make it worthwhile.

7. Limit private-life sharing. We are writers who hustle, who have families and responsibilities, and it's expected that life will get in the way. A mastermind group can become a safe space to share difficult problems you may be facing at work and, at times, in your personal life too. But be careful about oversharing or taking up too much time venting about your personal problems. This isn't the place, and these aren't the people for that. Yes, they are here to support you, but unless they specifically ask to know more, it's often a good idea to keep private matters private. As the group grows and you get to know each other more, there may be more space for sharing the personal stuff.

8. Be a good listener. Be mindful. Be open-minded, supportive, and encouraging. And walk away if the group isn't for you, or for this time in your life. You can exit a group gracefully, with gratitude and goodwill. There's nothing wrong with realizing that it's not a good fit. Honoring your own boundaries and learning when to say no are important parts of successful networking. You can't say yes to every path, and trying to do so frequently leads to frustration.

When you start a mastermind group, it's good for each member to do a "business inventory," which is a snapshot of where they are in their business and where they want to be by year's end. Members share this information with the group and devise individual steps (or building blocks) that will contribute to each goal. Once everyone has established their goals and intermediate steps/strategies, the group can schedule regular quarterly (or weekly, or monthly) goal reviews where everyone checks in and shares what they've accomplished so far—and what they still have on their to-do lists.

Though this sounds like a streamlined process, depending on how much time the group has and the approach that makes sense for the members, it's possible that much of the early self-assessment, goal setting, and strategizing might be done as a group, with a lot of back-and-forth and opportunities to give and get feedback. This is particularly helpful for newer authors. Other mastermind groups might have more experienced members who are set on their goals and next steps and who really just need accountability partners. Discussing and setting expectations before embarking on the group mastermind journey will help everyone get on the same page and make sure their communication and learning styles mesh.

Here's a sample of what our mastermind group meeting agenda looks like:

1. News or successes ("wins") since last call

2. Progress report on goals from last call

3. Discussion topic of the week (e.g., three top-priority goals, author platform challenges, ARC readers, book marketing, webinars we are taking/conferences we are attending for continuing education)

4. Requests for backup (e.g., asking for support or reality checks)

5. Scheduling next call

The Broad, Dispersed Network

If our small, trusted network gives us depth and substance, the broad, dispersed network gives us reach. There will be overlap between our small and broad networks, but we can distinguish between them by focusing on how we'll interact with each group and the kind of benefits we'll give and potentially receive depending on the nature of the network.

This expanded network consists of people we may only know online—people we follow and interact with on a larger, less personal level (like peers on a discussion list, a subject matter expert we just found on Discord or Instagram, a prominent author on Facebook, an indie publisher on LinkedIn). We're able to relate to them because we share common goals and are in a similar industry (or industries that complement each other), but we don't know the person in real life and haven't had extensive communication with them online.

This loosely connected network is made up of individuals—and communities—we interact with without being particularly intimate or vulnerable—it's a wider net of diverse contacts. Yes, they are more superficial at first—because we haven't developed relationships yet—but they enrich our perspective and also give us a chance to make connections beyond our everyday relationships. As we get to know members of this broad network, we'll look for opportunities to deepen our exchanges and perhaps meet offline—at conferences, for coffee, or in other meetups. And if we're networking with the goal of gaining new clients, or readers, *the more people who know that we're a writer, the better.*

This extended network is a great place to both learn and teach (in other words, share our knowledge and build our reputation for expertise—and approachability). While our close network mainly consists of people we have much in common with, the wide network is where we go to expand our boundaries or to conduct research that's beyond the perspective of our immediate network. Just as writing can be isolating, at times the writing community can be insular. Reaching out beyond our usual sources of information helps us stay informed, open-minded, and inclusive. And for a writer, these qualities are critical to success.

A WRITER'S PERSPECTIVE

Networking seemed somewhat unnecessary to me from the relative security of a full-time job for a publishing company in Mexico. But jobs don't last forever, and personal priorities change: organizing your agenda, being your own boss, spending more time on the things that matter to you, and, yes, starting from zero when a pandemic devastates the economy and takes away "nonessential" businesses. My search for new horizons in the United States—a market with sixty million Spanish speakers—led me to various associations for publishing professionals. It was there that I discovered the value of networking: sharing experiences, knowledge, and projects with other authors. Without being a full-time writer yet, I realized the importance of stepping out of the full-time employee comfort zone.

—LUIS ARTURO PELAYO, SPANISH TO MOVE

INSIGHT: NOTES ON AUDIENCE

As I mentioned earlier, for much of this workbook we don't make a distinction between networking with writing peers and networking with potential clients, vendors, publishers, or readers (thinking "book clubs" here). Today especially, so many of our interactions are public—or publicly available—that targeting specific audiences with specific messages can be difficult. There's a lot of overlap, and it's especially important to present a cohesive brand presence, regardless of your audience.

For this reason, we recommend that authors be circumspect with how they present themselves and how they talk about readers, clients, competitors, and peers in virtual and real-life spaces. There are places and times that are appropriate for venting or sharing potentially embarrassing information, such as in a secure space with close, trusted colleagues. But remember that the world at large isn't a safe space. There are trolls and others who will judge harshly and harass freely simply because they can, because it feeds the less-pleasant instincts of human nature. And there are potential publishers who don't need to know their writer's particular life circumstances unless the writer chooses to share the information with them. The point here is be *intentional* about what you share. And keep in mind that *the intended* audience isn't the same as *the actual* audience.

Figuring out how open or private to be online, especially as a writer, is a challenging and personal decision. What works for some of us won't work for others, so I'm not going to give specific recommendations beyond what I've said already. But for an insightful take on what you can be doing differently, I've found the podcast and book marketing and social media guides from Jenn Hanson-dePaula from Mixtus Media incredibly valuable.

Another consideration regarding audience is deciding what information and assistance to give away without charging for it (as when mentoring a newbie or helping a member of a close network), and what constitutes billable work. As with most everything in the writing world, this is a personal business decision. As part of my community-mindedness, I've often spent a fair amount of time helping peers (reviewing outlines, discussing book or chapter titles, reviewing blurbs or blog posts, advising on language, etc.), but I've found that when dealing with vendors, clients, or readers, it's often wise to be diligent about boundaries, especially where project scope and fair compensation are concerned. In each case, regardless of who the audience is, it's important to remember that relationship building is the foundation of networking, and to build real relationships, it's necessary to be honest, set expectations, and maintain healthy boundaries.

EVALUATE YOUR CURRENT NETWORK

How do we decide where to find our broad network connections? That's coming up in chapter 3: Networking Goals. But first, let's use the worksheets at the end of this chapter to evaluate our starting point: the small/trusted and broad/dispersed networks we have right now.

Think about who is currently in each network, and who you would like to have in your network. Is your trusted network solid, but do you seldom venture out of it? Or are you in all the places, meeting all the people, while sensing that what you really need are a few trusted colleagues you can talk to with a greater degree of openness?

Use the following exercises to help visualize your current networks so you can gain perspective and have a better idea of the nature and depth of your web of professional relationships *today*. After all, to form a plan for where we want to go (and how to get there), we must first know where we're starting out.

In the worksheets, make note of

People: Who are you interacting with? (People are key because relationships are key!)

Platform: What medium do you interact with them on? (Text messaging? Slack space? Email? Circle? Vox? Local writers' meetup? Conference? Phone? Zoom? Instagram? LinkedIn? Facebook? Discord?)

Industry: What area do they move in/gravitate to (which is, hopefully, an industry that you draw business from)? This might be a specific community (indie contemporary romance authors, PhD candidates in the social sciences, corporate HR or marketing clients, niche academics, bookstores) or a particular specialty within the publishing industry (acquisitions editors, cover designers, permissions editors, technical editors, book coaches, translators, book launch specialists, formatters, indexers, sensitivity readers).

After you fill out the following worksheets,[1] take a few minutes to evaluate what you find. Do most of your close connections come from a single source—a previous employer, a specific professional organization, a niche writing group? If so, what benefit might there be in cultivating strong relationships with people outside those groups (not to replace your trusted network, but to broaden it)?

For instance, if most of your close connections are from a previous in-house job, that's probably a comfortable, safe space—and possibly a great source of business. But sudden changes in that company's management or direction might leave you floundering, especially if your close network is too narrow (I can't tell you how many times I've seen this happen). By putting your current networks (small *and* broad) on paper, you can identify patterns and gaps that need filling that might not stand out otherwise.

Take this opportunity to find both the strengths and the areas for improvement (via expansion or deepening) in your current network. Maybe there are types of contacts you're missing and need to add. (For example, if you're a writer who networks mainly with indie authors, you'll be able to better serve your colleagues if you can offer trusted recommendations for cover designers, editors, or beta readers.) When considering your broad, dispersed network, in particular, don't underestimate the many connections you already have. Part of being a successful freelancer or indie author is finding opportunities in the unlikeliest of places.

---

1   Keep in mind that the worksheets throughout this book provide snapshots of where you are today and will evolve as you develop your networking strategy. You'll revisit them as you continue to develop your strategy and abilities.

Self-Assessment Worksheet: Current Network Snapshot

MY SMALL, TRUSTED NETWORK

My current small, trusted network is made up of the people listed below. I know I can go to them with questions, doubts, ideas, or success stories, and that I will receive their honest feedback.

PERSON	PLATFORM	INDUSTRY/SPECIALTY REPRESENTED

Questions: Whom is my network missing?
              What does this tell me about my preferred platform?
              Am I networking exclusively in one niche?

Self-Assessment Worksheet: Current Network Snapsho

MY BROAD NETWORK

My current broad network is made up of the people listed below. I may not know all of these connections personally, but they are in my orbit and help broaden my understanding and reach.

PERSON	PLATFORM	INDUSTRY/SPECIALTY REPRESENTED
_____	_____	_____
_____	_____	_____
_____	_____	_____
_____	_____	_____
_____	_____	_____
_____	_____	_____
_____	_____	_____
_____	_____	_____
_____	_____	_____
_____	_____	_____
_____	_____	_____
_____	_____	_____
_____	_____	_____
_____	_____	_____
_____	_____	_____

Questions: Whom is my network missing?
What does this tell me about my preferred platform?
Am I networking exclusively in one niche?
Is my network shallow and disjointed?

Place the worksheets side by side and notice how they compare. Are your two networks balanced in terms of the number of contacts and the industries represented? Or is your overall (combined) network shallow and disjointed? Is the focus too narrow? Too broad? Make some preliminary notes and hold on to these worksheets. We'll revisit them in chapter 10.

For those who prefer a spatial/visual approach, you might try using the mind map method instead of the list worksheets. Here are two examples of how to map your broad network, with some starter connections.

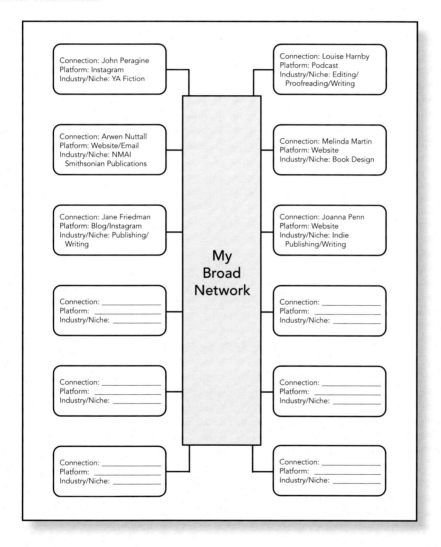

Broad network practice mind map for book writers.

This next example is a bit more niche, just to show you the level of detail a writer for academic journals might have when completing their mind map. How your map will be built depends on who you write for (or want to write for). And as you grow and evolve as a writer, so might your projects and goals. So the mind map you create today will be different than the one you complete five years from now because you will be at a different stage in your career.

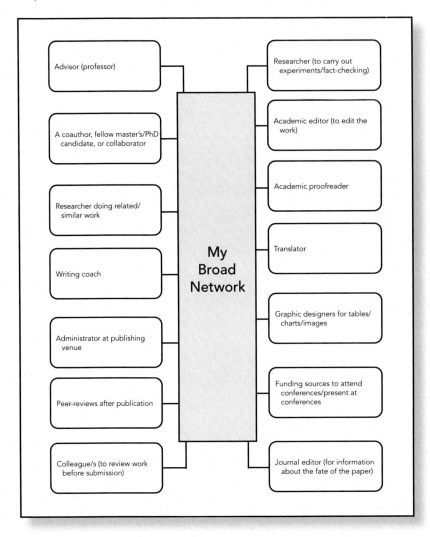

Broad network practice mind map for academic journal writers.

After you've filled out these snapshots (or constructed your network mind maps) and have a better understanding of your current networks, move on to chapter 3, where we'll work on developing your networking goals. Then we'll dive into chapter 4, where we'll identify who you need to reach out to as you pursue those goals.

CHAPTER 3

NETWORKING GOALS

The best way to overcome our resistance to networking is to clarify our networking goals. Then, have a "WIN" attitude. Identify and only focus on "What's Important Now."

—BRITTANY DOWDLE & LINDA RUGGERI, THE NETWORKING STUDIO

Why network? Short answer: to help us achieve our goals and find solutions to our challenges. The accepted wisdom is that networking is something we should all be doing. It's touted as a magic key in advice like "It's not what you know, it's *who* you know." But often we approach this important activity with unfocused intentions and an unclear understanding of how to do it "right" and how it will help us. The line between effort and return on investment is nebulous at best.

Carolyn See devotes a whole chapter to "Hang Out with People Who Support Your Work," in her book *Making a Literary Life*, because it can get very lonely and very negative out there when you're a writer without a community. It truly helps to be surrounded by others who want to see us thrive and support us along the way, but we don't always know where or how to find them.

Though we know networking is something we're *supposed* to do, many of us are uncomfortable when it's time to actually get out there and "network." This discomfort may come from social anxiety, or from the dread of being viewed as pushy or characterized as trying to "monetize" our relationships.

As an indie author and freelance editor who works at home by myself, I know we also run the risk of living, as my Argentine family calls it, "inside our ravioli."[2] We lock ourselves up in our own little space, solely interact with a screen (or two), maybe even our cats or dogs, and clatter away at our keyboard all day. It's a haven; it's what we know; it's where eight hours can go by in the blink of an eye. But it's also isolating, and we can quickly lose touch

---

2   In Argentina we also say "inside a thermos" or "inside a Tupper" (for Tupperware).

with reality, with new industry trends, with the big picture. It's easy to become hyperfocused and neglect our place in the writing community. And when that happens, we can miss out on opportunities, on catching up with colleagues, on learning about contests, submissions, classes, or conferences—or even on meeting new potential readers at a book event who are looking for writers like us.

The resistance shows up as that little voice that says, *I don't have time to network. Is it really worth it? No one's interested in my perspective—I don't have anything interesting to say or share.*

To counter these thoughts, first we'll **identify what we want to accomplish with our networking**. In other words, what is the *goal* networking can help us achieve? Why network?

Having measurable, well-defined goals will focus our efforts so we can network with intention. When we identify these goals (our destination), networking becomes the path between where we are today and that destination. (But remember, the destination we're working toward isn't the final stop on our professional journey—it's simply the next step.)

Let's start by reviewing some of the main reasons writers network. At the bottom of the following list, there are a few extra bullet points for you to fill out in case I've missed goals that are important to you. (If you notice that some of these goals overlap, you're right!)

Writers network...

- to build long-term reader relationships (superfans)
- to build long-term colleague relationships
- to get more readers or clients or reach new markets
- to diversify our writing portfolios (and keep our work interesting)
- to establish a reputation
- to build a brand
- to increase revenue through new opportunities (i.e., "going wide")
- to be part of a community

- to learn from colleagues
- to help colleagues (by sharing what we know)
- to be part of the conversation and stay relevant
- to improve our skills
- to develop new skills
- to stay informed of industry best practices and trends
- _____
- _____

Which of these goals are most important to you *at this point in your writer journey?*

In case the list is too overwhelming—you probably want to accomplish all of these goals right now—let's meet some authors who also need to identify their most pressing business needs (a.k.a. goals) and how networking can help them succeed.

Writer Snapshot (Needs and Goals)

Meet Adie, the new-to-writing writer:

Adie has just started working on her first book, a mystery, after completing a writing certificate program, and her goal is **to self-publish her first book and to connect with more indie myster writers and readers,** so she decides to focus on **establishing her reputation** and **building her readership and brand.** Many other excellent reasons for networking may feed into her primary goal, but she can't do everything at once, so she's decided to focus on this multipart goal.

Adie's main goal: to connect with more indie mystery writers and readers

Adie's substep goals:

- establish a reputation
- build a brand

Meet Jaden, the new-to-freelancing copywriter:

Jaden has worked in-house for corporate companies, but now she's going freelance, and the transition is stressful. She already has some great connections in marketing, but she needs to learn more about the business side of freelancing, so Jaden's networking goal is **to build a successful freelance career** by **learning business best practices from colleagues** and **establishing a freelance reputation.**

Jaden's main goal: build a freelance career

Jaden's substep goals:

- learn freelancing business skills
- establish a freelance reputation
- create a copywriter resume

Meet Parker, the established podcast writer trying to increase their income:

Parker has built a satisfying career first writing for TV, and now writing on a podcast team, but they need **to be more profitable**. This might mean creating new income streams, working more efficiently, or changing their mindset around money. There are so many possibilities, but they're going to have to narrow their focus. Parker is in a stable place financially, so they decide to take their time and network with other writers—outside of podcasting—to find out how others have met this challenge.

Parker's main goal: be more profitable

Parker's *possible* substep goals:

- identify new income streams (coaching journalists, teaching writing classes, creating workshops, doing presentations, etc.)
- change money mindset (keep track of expenses, reduce overhead, set quarterly financial goals, invest funds for retirement, etc.)
- research and test more efficient writing practices for teaching classes/developing course curriculum
- learn public speaking skills/sharpen coaching skills
- try pitching a course idea to a continuing education program, explore a new writing niche, brainstorm prescriptive nonfiction book ideas based on expertise

Meet Alejandro, the fatigued indie writer:

Alejandro has published, sold, and produced plenty of work and has a solid reputation in his niche, but he's feeling isolated and stuck in his genre. He needs **to get out of his rut and into a more positive headspace**. Alejandro's networking goals are **to diversify his writing portfolio** and **to become part of an MG community**, so he has more support from MG writers who "get" him and can help him navigate this new work.

Alejandro's main goal: get out of his rut and into a more positive headspace

Alejandro's substep goals:

- diversify his writing portfolio
- become part of an MG writing community

Your Writer Snapshot (Needs and Goals)

Take a moment to evaluate your own situation. Do you identify with Adie, Jaden, Parker, or Alejandro? Or is your situation a bit different?

Without overthinking it, quickly fill out the following, placing yourself in the role of one of our writers:

I am (your name) _____, a (type of) _____ writer.

I have (current situation/experience) _____

_____,

but need (insert need/challenge) _____

_____.

To meet this need/fix this problem/change this situation, my goal is: _____

_____

_____

_____

_____

_____

_____

_____

To achieve this goal, I will focus on these substeps (list two networking goals that have the

potential to solve this challenge): _____

_____

_____

_____

_____

Now, set this aside for a moment and read on.

Setting Goals

Without a clear goal, our networking efforts are often inefficient and draining. We may eventually arrive at our destination, but the journey will likely take longer and be fraught with wrong turns and dead ends.

When my networking goals are undefined and my actions aren't moving me closer to achieving what I'm looking for, I've found that a good approach is to take a step back and make my goals *overt and specific*. That way, I'm in a better position to develop a solid, actionable plan instead of the usual scattered-pasta-against-the-wall plan so many of us default to while hoping for the best.

Whose Goals?

The first step when linking goals to our networking plan is to realize that our goals are unique and will change over time. Even though we're all writers, we don't all have the same goals. Why? Because we write in different genres and niches—with different specialties and skill sets. Because each one of us is at a different place in our career. Because we all have different responsibilities, needs, and life situations.

Some of us are just starting off in our writing careers, while some of us are midcareer, and others may be looking for a change of industry or clients. Some are looking to retire within a year and would like to work part-time, maybe changing their niche to align with their hobbies. Because we are individuals, our goals are different, and the beauty of networking is that no one goal or strategy applies to everyone. We get to set our goals and customize our path based on what works for us—based on what *need* we're working to fulfill today.

Let's take a moment to digest that idea: another person's goal may not fit *our* situation. It follows that the networking tactics they employ might not be the best choice for *our* goals. It's easy to be seduced by the shiny, sparkling wonder of someone else's goal-strategy journey. *They have it all figured out*, we think. *I just have to do everything they're doing, then I'll have made it.* To that, we say: By all means, study other people's successes, study their methods, analyze what resonates, and examine why it's working (e.g., their volunteer work builds community, their blog posts establish reputation/brand, their LinkedIn articles show their subject matter expertise). But always come back to your goals and base your networking plan on what *you need* to build the writing career *you* want.

Pause and give yourself permission to do some deep thinking about where your business is and where it's headed. Though foundational goal development is beyond the scope of this workbook, we want to emphasize that your networking strategy needs to be based on your business goals for it to be efficient and deliver the intended results. I've provided some additional resources in appendix B that can help you with goal setting. In the meantime, start where you are—follow your instincts and craft the starter goals that will move you in your intended direction.

Goal Time

Using the writer-snapshot exercise as a starting point, brainstorm the business goals that will help you get to the next level in your freelance career. There may not be one right answer, but rather a few serviceable answers that you must choose between.

Beginning from a macro level, jot down your main goal, and then brainstorm a few steps you can take that will help you achieve the main goal. For each goal that you set, ask yourself, *Is this goal measurable, achievable, and dependent on my own actions?*

For example, here's Jaden's goal map:

Main goal: Build a career as a copywriter

Step 1 to reach main goal → learn freelancing business skills
- substep: create proposal and contract template
- substep: start a website
- substep: learn about self-employment taxes
- substep: develop a vision for her business, establish its purpose, write a mission statement, values, and long-term goals

Step 2 to reach main goal → establish a freelance reputation
- substep: write ten blog posts (800 to 1200 words) about copywriting
- substep: send pitches/submission ideas
- substep: write four LinkedIn articles to publish one per month

Steps 3 to reach main goal → create a copywriter resume
- substep: create a copywriter bio
- substep: post bio on online directories

 Goals should be broad enough to give you room to grow, but narrow enough to give you direction—and a way to objectively evaluate whether you've hit them.

Next, use the space provided to elaborate on your main and secondary goals for your business.

My main goal for my business this year is: _____

_____

_____

Step 1 to reach main goal (supporting main goal)→ _____

_____

- substep: _____

- substep: _____

Step 2 to reach main goal (supporting main goal)→ _____

_____

- substep: _____

- substep: _____

Step 3 to reach main goal (supporting main goal→ _____

_____

- substep: _____

- substep: _____

BRINGING IT ALL TOGETHER:
THE QUARTERLY NETWORKING WORKSHEET

Now that you've established your top business goals, you can begin to fill out the Quarterly Networking Worksheet by inserting these goals into the first section. The purpose of condensing your networking plan into one sheet is to give you a high-level summary that you can print out and keep close by. This worksheet is important because it will help you

- organize your thoughts,
- create a plan,

- position yourself to get results, and
- evaluate your successes at the end of each quarter.

There will be a lot of people we'll start connecting with once we have a clear idea of our goals. And we'll figure out what is the best way to connect with them in subsequent chapters. But for now, based on your above goal(s) for this year, who do you need to reach now? Let's add that information to the Quarterly Networking Worksheet. For now only complete the first section (main goal, substep goals, and start date).

Quarterly Networking Worksheet

Start Date: _____

Main Goal: _____

Building-Block Substeps: _____

_____

_____

_____

Based on my networking goal(s) for this quarter, whom do I need to reach now? _____

_____

How can I use each Networking Tactic to reach them?

Action for My Website: _____

_____

Action for My Personal Communications: _____

_____

Action for My Social Media: _____

_____

Action for My Professional Organizations: _____

_____

Action for My Volunteer Activities: _____

_____

End-of-Quarter Networking Review

End Date: _____

Progress: _____

_____

_____

A WRITER'S PERSPECTIVE

For me, networking is about building relationships, for all the reasons one does that: to connect, to feel less alone, to seek support, and to get to know people who are similar and different from you. As someone who has been self-employed for over twenty years, this has been extra important, because I don't have an office of colleagues to run things by, or ask for support. This was also especially helpful during the early days of the pandemic when I lost a lot of work due to shutdowns. Networking helped me retain work and build connections that have made a huge difference in my business.

From a writing perspective, networking has helped me answer important questions about publishing and the writing process. It has introduced me to people who have been important in my writing journey, such as an agent or editor connection, and it has helped me to creatively solve problems within my writing. It has also led to work opportunities I would never have found on my own.

If you think of networking as building important relationships that you may still have for the rest of your career or life, I think it's easy to see why networking can be useful. Additionally, early on, networking can steer you in the right direction toward steps that are healthy for your career, and away from actions that aren't worth your time or worse.

—**JORDAN ROSENFELD,** AUTHOR OF *Fallout, Women in Red,* AND
Forged in Grace AND SIX BOOKS ON THE CRAFT OF WRITING

CHAPTER 4

USING GOALS TO IDENTIFY POTENTIAL NETWORKING PARTNERS

Your network is your net worth.

—*Porter Gale, author and entrepreneur*

People tend to work with, and refer, people they know and trust. So the first networking step is *becoming known*, and the second is *building trust*. Before you can do either, however, you need to identify who your ideal network is composed of—and where they can be found.

Now we'll use the goals from the previous chapter to determine who you need to reach and where you can find these networking partners. Take a look at your Current Network Snapshots (My Small Trusted Network, and My Broad Network) from chapter 2 (p. 28).

Does your combined network contain the people you need to connect with in order to reach your specific goals?

If not, it might be time to broaden your network or pursue a more specialized cohort of connections. Note, this isn't about dropping current contacts based on whether they are useful to you—that's transactional and contrary to maintaining real relationships. Instead, if your network is a mismatch for the direction you're trying to move in, then you need to expand your network in the direction of your desired growth. But keep those early connections! If you have a rapport with someone, don't squander it. Tomorrow's networks are built of yesterday's and today's relationships. And keep in mind that a significant part of networking is being there for others—being a strong support in someone else's network. That spirit of selfless support and giving is at the core of every effective networking relationship.

Writer Snapshot (People to Connect With)

Let's revisit our four writers to see who they might want to develop relationships with based on their goals:

Adie, the new-to-writing writer:

Adie's main goal: to connect with more indie mystery writers and readers

Adie's substep goals:

- establish a reputation
- build a brand

Adie needs to connect with (general): mystery readers and writers; new indie authors who can offer community, learning opportunities, and referrals. Where are they active?

Adie needs to connect with (specific): an indie author community within the mystery genre; indie publishers who specialize in working with indie authors—in particular, those who offer editing in her genre, such as developmental editing; organizations that support indie authors; Facebook groups where indie authors congregate to discuss craft, marketing, cross-promotion; professional writing associations; bloggers who curate writing resources for writers. Where are they active?

Jaden, the new-to-freelancing copywriter:

Jaden's main goal: build a freelance career

Jaden's substep goals:

- learn freelancing business skills
- establish a freelance reputation
- create a copywriter resume

Jaden needs to connect with (general): companies who need copywriting services, freelance writers who can offer community and share experiences (and lessons learned). Where are they active?

Jaden needs to connect with (specific): professional writing associations, informal writing groups (perhaps on Facebook), freelance communities (like the Freelancers Union), instructors specializing in the business of writing, SCORE (the Service Corps of Retired Executives), copywriting instructors. Where are they active?

Parker, the established podcast writer trying to increase their income:

Parker's main goal: be more profitable

Parker's *possible* substep goals:

- identify new income streams (coaching journalists, teaching writing classes, creating workshops, doing presentations, etc.)

- change money mindset (keep track of expenses, reduce overhead, set quarterly financial goals, invest funds for retirement, etc.)

- research and test more efficient writing practices for teaching classes/developing course curriculum

- learn public speaking skills/sharpen coaching skills

- try pitching a course idea to a continuing education program, explore a new writing niche, brainstorm prescriptive nonfiction book ideas based on expertise

Parker needs to connect with (general): writers or authors at similar stages of their careers, authors in other genres or niches, writers who are open to new ways of practicing their craft or to collaborations. Where are they active?

Parker needs to connect with (specific): professional writing associations; university extension programs; productivity specialists (in writing and in freelancing); mindset coaches; writers who use specific writing software or mailing list management software; writers in related niches that might be more profitable; niche writers who offer coaching, online classes, etc. Where are they active?

Alejandro, the fatigued indie writer:

Alejandro's main goal: get out of his rut and into a more positive headspace

Alejandro's substep goals:

- diversify his writing portfolio
- become part of an MG community

Alejandro needs to connect with (general): clients who need his specific specialty, but whose business model or content is different from his current client roster; clients who are in adjacent industries; clients who offer short projects with quick turnaround times, as opposed to current clients who have massive projects; writing groups. Where are they active?

Alejandro needs to connect with (specific): niche industry groups whose members are potential clients; writing organizations and groups that have community-minded goals (like the Nonfiction Authors Association), where Alejandro can get to know others, interact, and share his knowledge; writing groups with peers who are at similar points in their careers or who share Alejandro's specialty. Where are they active?

As these examples show, different writers may develop relationships with widely divergent groups based on their specific goals. Academic writers will need to reach different kinds of clients and colleagues than screenwriters, who will need different connections than billionaire-romance authors, who will need an altogether different network than technical writers or copywriters. And even within the broader content genres, each writing professional may need to network in distinctive ecosystems. For instance, the networking plan of a spy thriller writer is going to differ from that of a YA writer who specializes in grimdark fantasy.

But we'll also have some overlap, generally in industry groups like the Society of Children's Book Writers and Illustrators (SCBWI) or in Facebook writing groups. In my experience, these large groups are great places to start, but many of our most valuable connections will be found in the smaller niche groups where we can really get to know people and form relationships. This is true for both developing industry connections and connecting with potential clients. So, my recommendation is to begin with the wide groups, then, through daily and weekly interaction, start to build relationships with people who have similar interests, specialties, skill sets, and goals. (More on this in chapter 6.)

Once you identify who you'd like to have in your network (in general or specific people/roles), then you can work on becoming known (a.k.a. using your website and social media for networking purposes, for example) and building trust (a.k.a. helping others find their own answers, sharing your knowledge, encouraging others).

Your Writer Snapshot (People to Connect With)

Using the information from the previous chapter (main goals, substeps for goals), let's look more into the people you need to connect with and where they are.

Here is a short list to give you some ideas of people you might want to be connecting with if you plan on being successful in the writing or publishing industry:

- Accessibility tester for all work published digitally
- Accountant with self-employment industry experience
- Agent
- Attorney with publishing industry experience
- Editor (developmental editors, line editors, copyeditors)
- Fact-checker
- Illustrator
- International rights expert
- Marketing consultant
- Other writers in your genre or trade
- Photographer
- Proofreader
- Publisher (traditional, indie, hybrid, magazine, literary reviews, journals)
- Publishing organizations
- Sensitivity/authenticity reader
- Social media manager
- Translator
- Website designer (hopefully with great SEO experience, see chapter 5)
- Writing organizations

Although we'd like to have all of these experts in our close network, let's focus on who is important to know *now*. The first three lines are an example to get you started.

People I Need to Connect With

Area of expertise

1. book cover designer

2. indexer

3. nonfiction copyeditor

4.

5.

6.

7.

8.

9.

10.

Name of person

1. Melinda Martin

2. Heather Pendley

3. Kelly Young

4.

5.

6.

7.

8.

9.

10.

Where they are active

1. Website, Facebook

2. Editorial Freelancers Association

3. Website, LinkedIn

4.

5.

6.

7.

8.

9.

10.

Spend some time brainstorming about who can help you reach your current goals. Look past the obvious choices and get creative. You can always dial back your reach, but start by giving yourself the space to imagine whose insights you'd love to have. Who is an expert you'd like to talk to? Who is already doing your dream project? Write down names, organizations, conferences, and social media spaces.

For example, maybe, like Adie, you want to connect with more indie authors of fiction. First jot down a category (indie authors), then narrow it down (indie authors who write mystery), then get specific (indie mystery authors who are members of Sisters in Crime or who participate in a Facebook mystery authors' group), then identify a few leading indie mystery authors and write down their names.

A quick note: It's not that you're going to email every best-selling indie mystery author and ask to be their best friend. You *are* going to follow them online, see where they hang out, what author groups they interact with, how they are attracting readers, what content they are sharing/writing, and what's important to them.

As you get a feel for that community of indie mystery authors, you'll begin to interact with others and later on, contribute what you know. First, you might learn more about the craft, or make connections with other writers who might be putting together projects you can contribute to (i.e., an anthology). You might learn tips on how to send out pitches or proposals to agents or publishers. Perhaps you become savvy about the pros and cons of self-publishing. Or you find a group of writers that helps you stay accountable to your weekly writing count goals. This type of networking can build your genre knowledge base, help you create a reputation (for example, as a writer who shares what they've discovered by providing resources for beginning mystery writers). In turn, developing this networking practice could help you

1. establish your reputation as a knowledgeable and approachable writer, and

2. build your author brand and position yourself as an expert within your genre or specialty.

Of course, this is an abbreviated version of the networking process, but you'll be ready to move on to more targeted activities in the next chapters, which focus on the specific networking tactics that form the structure of your networking plan.

A WRITER'S PERSPECTIVE

The biggest challenge facing indie authors is the lack of industry connections that traditional publishers have. Successful networking is the clear way to bridge this gap. Building genuine relationships with other people in the publishing industry—writers, editors, designers, subject matter experts, and beyond—will help you sell more books and have more fun while you're at it.

In my line of work, I have found the information from Writer Beware and from the Science Fiction and Fantasy Writers Association (SFWA) to be indispensable.

—**KATHERINE PICKETT,** OWNER OF POP EDITORIAL SERVICES LLC
AND AUTHOR OF *Perfect Bound: How to Navigate
the Book Publishing Process Like a Pro*

PART 2

NETWORKING TACTICS

So far, we've defined *networking*, evaluated your current network, identified your most pressing networking goals, and considered who to network with to support those goals. As I said at the beginning of this workbook, to network successfully, we must prepare to network. So now that we have the foundation down, let's turn to the tools and tactics we need to have in place to support and build our ideal network.

CHAPTER 5

NETWORKING TACTIC #1
A WEBSITE

A website will promote you 24/7: No employee will do that.

—PAUL COOKSON, MARKETING CONSULTANT

When you start a literary career, at some point—and usually sooner than later—someone will ask you where they can find your work online. And if you don't have a website they can easily access or find, you most likely just lost a potential reader, who could have recommended your work to many other readers. What's more, your website is one of the few public things about your work that these days you *can* control.

If people like your work, they'll start following you on social media. They will want to know when your next project is coming out, what other things you're writing about, what books you recommend, who you like to read, and so much more. A website is a safe space where you cannot only share that information, but also an additional place to sell your work and build a following, like by capturing email addresses for a future newsletter or email blast showcasing your next project.

Writer and author websites have evolved significantly over the last few years. Now you can even monetize your work further by selling products (books, courses, companion guides, merchandise) directly on your website using an e-commerce platform like Shopify, and scale it as your business grows (however, if this is the route you choose to go, make sure to study up beforehand for best results).

WEBSITE AS NETWORKING TOOL

When new writers ask me what they should focus on early in their careers, I always recommend to focus first on continuing education—and then, a website. Unless you're a veteran writer with a deep network that has consistently brought you more business than you can handle for years on end, you probably need a website.

Your website is the professional version of *you*, but on the internet. In old-school business terms, it's a storefront. But for writers, it has the potential to be so much more! Just as you would introduce yourself to a prospective reader in person (stating who you are, what you do, telling them what you write about—basically, laying the foundation for a business relationship), a website is one way we replicate that experience on the internet. It's a chance for anyone with internet access, anywhere in the world, to meet you and begin to develop a sense of what type of writer you are and how you write.

But how exactly does having a website serve your networking efforts? A website gives you a place (that you own) where you can do things like

- Share samples of work through short posts about what you are writing (previews)

- Share your knowledge via a blog or articles (thereby establishing your expertise or passion, and creating organic opportunities for interacting with visitors)

- Curate downloadable/printable resources, that complement your writing work, for peers and potential clients (showing that you're knowledgeable, while helping others solve their own challenges)

- Establish credibility through testimonials or reviews

- Define your brand (from tone to niche to voice and visual brand markers)

- Show that you're a real person, not a computer solely running on AI on an uninhabited island

- Share samples of work of other authors you help or collaborate with, if you have the authors' permission (this is a great way to cross-promote each other)

- Talk about your writing in detail (positioning yourself within your industry/genre, so visitors can tell at a glance what you do)

- Highlight your specialty, genre, or niche (if you have one)

- Communicate in your unique voice

There's overlap and interconnectedness in almost everything we do as writers, so it's no surprise that a website can be a networking tool, a marketing tool, a sales tool, and much more.

That's why I'm encouraging you to think about how your website can *specifically* support you as you *prepare to network*.

By having a website that tells your story and positions you within the writing community, delineating your skills, projects, and specialties, you'll be ready to benefit from all the other networking you're already doing.

For example, let's say Renna, another of our writing colleagues, attends a conference and another writer, Jae, is impressed by her knowledge on world-building and her professional attitude, so they want to add her to their collaborator list. As soon as they get back from the conference, they look her up online. She has a TikTok account, but no website. Or perhaps she has a website, but it's geared toward a very different genre from what she's currently specializing in (for example, Renna's website describes her as a real estate copywriter, but she told Jae that her current focus is on writing flash noir).

This puts Jae in an awkward position. They believe that Renna would do a great job on whatever project she takes on, but they also know that it won't work to suggest Renna to the other writers on the project. The writers will question both Renna's suitability for the project and Jae's judgment (or listening skills) for recommending her. This one disconnect—having a website that doesn't align with her goals (or having no website)—sabotages Renna's investment in the conference and potentially undermines her relationship with Jae. This is a made-up scenario, but it's based on my observations of "connections gone awry" (which unfortunately is more common than we'd wish).

This is why I view our websites as one of the first foundational tools in my approach to networking. Whether you're updating an existing site or creating a whole new website, you'll use the primary goals and substep goals we identified earlier to shape your website's focus and message.

For example, revisiting our colleagues from chapter 3, Adie might add a curated resources page and monthly blog to help establish her reputation and build her brand. In her "About Me" section, Jaden might highlight her corporate copywriting experience with New York clients and let visitors know that she's now offering freelance copywriting, which gives marketing or branding agencies access to a New York writer. Parker might use their website to sell a digital toolkit, conduct an online technical podcast writing course, or book speaking engagements with writer associations. And Alejandro might host an "ask the writer" blog geared toward helping new writers entering his niche, which can help him build relationships with other writers who appreciate his expertise while also showing potential publishers the depth of his knowledge in their specific subject matter.

Each of these activities helps the writer become known to both peers and potential readers and clients, and each activity contributes to building the trust that's at the base of every relationship.

> *Seventy-five percent of users admit to making judgments about a company's credibility based on their website's design.*
>
> —STANFORD WEB CREDIBILITY RESEARCH

ASSESS OR CREATE YOUR WEBSITE

Assess

If you have a website already but are haunted by the sinking feeling (or outright evidence) that it's not representing you well, a first step is to do a quick online search with a few keywords that you feel fit your profile, and then notice which other writers' websites come up. (Warning, this is where impostor syndrome can creep in! The purpose of this exercise isn't to make you feel "less than," but to gain a constructive perspective by visiting the sites of writers who offer similar services or indie authors that publish in the same genre.)

Experience those sites first as a potential client or reader. Take note of visceral reactions to the color scheme, the aesthetic, the fonts, the use of imagery, and the organization. Do you instantly trust this writer and the product they put out? Do you immediately question their professionalism? Are you filled with excitement or bored before you even start reading? Can you tie these emotional reactions to specific stylistic aspects of the website, regardless of the text?

Now experience the sites wearing your "businessperson" hat. And remember to view these surface aspects of each website through the lens of networking. After all, if you're trying to build relationships with visitors to your site (whether peers, clients, or readers), your site's "vibe" is important. Quite often we make instant decisions based on instinct. Pay attention to the sites that impressed you as professional, confidence inspiring, and interesting. From a visual standpoint, what do those sites have in common?

Now flip to your website. It's hard to be impartial, but try to separate yourself from the words (and the fact that it's your site) and just notice the same visual cues—color scheme, aesthetic, fonts, imagery, organization. What does your site have in common with the sites you liked (in your guise of "potential client")? What does it have in common with the sites that made you react with a "meh" or "no way!"? Take notes and maybe even print out screenshots of your landing page and the other sites' landing pages for comparison.

Next, list the pages (menu choices) that the sites have in common. How are the pages grouped? Is the flow logical to you as a potential client? Or does it feel more focused on the writer and less on your user experience?

Now go back to your site. Is it missing any pages that all the other websites have? Does it have a lot of additional menu choices? There isn't one right way to organize your website or a perfect number of pages, but there are best practices that provide a useful range for meeting most needs. (More on this in a bit.)

In this exercise, the goal is to 1) find websites of writers who share your expertise and niche, 2) evaluate how well their websites are working and note the observable aspects of their sites, and 3) use that information to reassess your own site. By taking notes and focusing on the quantifiable, objective aspects of the sites that inspire confidence and make you want to work with or read those writers, you can then apply those same techniques to your own site. Just remember, *never* copy or use someone else's content without their explicit permission. Creativity has no limits, so do your best to be *you* on your website.

And let me add a note on AI here. If you're going to try your hand at using AI for this, remember that AI is the simulation of human intelligence processes by machines. It will never capture who you really are or your essence as a writer. What's more, AI-generated text isn't protected by copyright. There are many people and technologies who can write similarly to you, or write the same types of books you write, but your work will be a unique product of your style, experience, and approach. This is what sets you apart. So, make it easy on yourself and your potential readers or customers by giving them the opportunity to get a sense of the person behind the writing.

> *People assign more credibility to sites that show they have been recently updated or reviewed.*
>
> —Stanford Web Credibility Research

Self-Assessment Worksheet: Website

Step 1: Your website

Website URL: _____

Editing services (examples: proofreading, line editing, ghostwriting, indexing):

_____

Genre/specialty (self-help, memoir, humanities textbooks, medical journals):

_____

Main site and font colors: _____

Main font styles: _____

_____

_____

_____

Images used: _____

_____

Page categories: _____

Professionalism: 1   2   3   4   5   6   7   8   9   10

Ease of navigation: _____

Call to action: _____

Ease of contact: 1   2   3   4   5   6   7   8   9   10

Editor-centric or client-centric approach? _____

Instant emotional reaction (from "I would work with this person" to "Meh" to "No way!")

          1   2   3   4   5   6   7   8   9   10

Self-Assessment Worksheet: Website

Step 2: Websites for editors offering the same services in the same genre/ specialty (choose five and complete the following exercise for each)

Website URL: _____

Editing services (examples: proofreading, line editing, ghostwriting, indexing):

_____

Genre/specialty (self-help, memoir, humanities textbooks, medical journals):

_____

Main site and font colors: _____

Main font styles: _____

_____

_____

_____

Images used: _____

_____

Page categories: _____

Professionalism: 1   2   3   4   5   6   7   8   9   10

Ease of navigation: _____

Call to action: _____

Ease of contact: 1   2   3   4   5   6   7   8   9   10

Editor-centric or client-centric approach? _____

Instant emotional reaction (from "I would work with this person" to "Meh" to "No way!")

                    1   2   3   4   5   6   7   8   9   10

Self-Assessment Worksheet: Website

Step 3: Compare and contrast

Which site do you like the most? The least? Why? _____

_____

_____

Which site is confidence inspiring? Why?_____

_____

_____

Which creates excitement about the prospect of working together? How?

_____

_____

What do the top two sites have in common? _____

_____

_____

What do the bottom two have in common? _____

_____

_____

How can you apply the lessons from the most engaging sites to the development or revision of your own site? _____

_____

_____

_____

_____

Create

Maybe you don't have a website at all. You've gotten by for years without one. To tell the truth, you've tried to create one a couple of times, but it just hasn't worked out. You're still writing, though, so—is it really necessary?

That depends. Are you content with the writing career and professional support network you have today? Are you confident they will be there for you tomorrow too? If there's a chance you could be doing better—more satisfying work, better writing opportunities, more book sales, making more money, or being part of a supportive writing community—then, yes. Let's build that website. It's not too hard. And it doesn't have to be expensive.

Creating a website isn't rocket science. Today many services will do everything for you for a minimal investment. With these services, you can create a basic and attractive website in one to two hours. If you don't have a website, and don't have the time to create one with the four basic pages ("Home," "Services," "Testimonials," "Contact Information"), then consider at least having a one-page website (for now): a simple landing page for your business that tells your clients you are real.

Some tech-savvy writers love the experience of building their own site. Some of us started building our website on our own, using WordPress and watching YouTube videos. We learned how to add plug-ins, use widgets, and organize our content. It's really up to you to decide what your comfort zone is (time, budget, and an interest in learning something new).

A mistake many of us make when we build our first website is that we build it according to what *we* like, without considering what our *audience* is looking for. Your website has to be well presented and dynamic (adapting to mobile views); it needs to have good keywords for search engine optimization (SEO). It should be informative and to the point, conveying exactly **who you are, what you do, and how to get in touch with you.**

Yes, creating a website from scratch is a project, but it's a reflection of you and your work. Once your website is up and running, the regular time commitment is minimal, though it will need to be updated at least once a year to make sure the information is still accurate *and* relevant. And an updated website is indexed in Google, so your search rank can improve. We all change, as do our businesses. We're dynamic human beings, and the media that represents us should also be dynamic.

Website Checklist

Whether you're creating a new website or using the takeaways from the previous self-assessment worksheet to revise your existing site, there is a checklist you can follow on my website (www.theinsightfuleditor.com/blog) to make sure you have a solid site.

For now, let's review what good information architecture for a website looks like:

- Landing page/home page

  o Place company name (or your name) front and center.

  o Be sure to use your full business name.

  o Include an up-to-date profile picture.

  o Provide easy-to-find contact information and social media links, ensuring that they're visible and clickable (meaning if a person clicks on one, it will take them to that site, ideally opening to a new page).

  o Make sure the type of writing you do is front and center. (Don't make clients guess.)

  o Check that all the information above exactly matches what you have on your social media networks/business card/directory profiles, etc. Remember, consistency is key to brand recognition![3]

- Services page (if you need one)

  o Clearly state every service you offer and what each means or entails.

  o Don't list services you *don't* offer, or services you have no experience with.

  o Consider offering writing packages or customizable packages.

  o If you list your rates, make sure they are up to date. If you don't want to list your rates, a good practice could be stating "My rates are updated every year. Please contact me for a quote or proposal," or "My rates are based on the Editorial Freelancers Association's rates chart," (yes, they have freelance writing rates on

---

3   Note: If you don't freelance full-time, or if writing is a side job for you, it may be hard to have your social media or website match across all platforms. Just try to make sure it's as consistent as possible.

there too), with a clickable link to that page. If your rates are negotiable, state that as well. Clients want to know whether you can adapt your rates or offerings to meet their budget. (And if it's your policy to use a strict rate schedule, that's okay too. The idea here is to use your website to set client expectations.)

- Testimonials page

  o Include relevant testimonials from satisfied clients, book reviewers, influencers, or readers.

    - List the name of the client with a link to their website/project/book page/ etc. Include a photo of the client, if the client agrees.

  o List best testimonials first, or newest to oldest.

  o Make sure each testimonial reflects one of the services you offer.

- Contact page

  o List your name, pronouns, and preferred contact method.

  o If your email address is provided, make sure it's clickable. (Security note: consider having a dedicated writer email address that's just for your website visitors, and not your personal one. You want to keep each separate.)

  o If you use a form that the client needs to fill out, make sure it's working. (It's easy to test a contact form; remember to do so periodically.)

Once you've implemented these website basics and have designed your website as an effective networking tool, make sure to list it in your email signature line, on any online profile you keep with organizations or social media platforms, on your business cards, and on your book's copyright page. It's important that the "online you" can be easily found and that you're easy to connect with.

SEO

Search engine optimization is everything to a website. There is so much to say about SEO and how we can harness it for our websites that at times it feels like a rabbit hole we're afraid to enter, but we need to know about it if we want to be found online.

Because it's beyond the scope of this book, I won't go into detail about SEO, but do inform yourself, learn about it, and maybe even take a class. For example, editor and author Michelle Lowery has years of valuable experience in this arena and offers an excellent class on SEO.

A WRITER'S PERSPECTIVE

Though it's called "search engine optimization," you're never creating content for search engines. You create content for people—your readers, colleagues, clients, and everyone in between. Those people just need to be able to find you, and they'll often use a search engine to do that, making SEO crucial to your business. If you find SEO intimidating, think of it as 'search experience optimization.' Give everyone who finds your content a positive experience: use natural-sounding language; make your content helpful, valuable, and accessible; relate to your audience, and help them relate to you; and yes, place your keywords in key spots (title tag, header tags, body copy, alt text). Do all that, and your content will be optimized for readers, which will by default make it pretty well optimized for search.

—MICHELLE LOWERY, SEO CONTENT STRATEGIST, SEVILLANA PUBLISHING, LLC

INSIGHT: ACCESSIBILITY

Whether you're designing your website, posting a link to your latest blog post, or uploading a video to TikTok or Instagram, take a moment to consider how to reach as many people as possible—while creating a space that *welcomes* as many people as possible. After all, social media is a tool for building community (and networking), and for it to be effective, we need to invite people in rather than shutting them out. We need to make sure that we're not perpetuating barriers that will keep anyone away from our writing. A good way to do this is by learning about accessibility tools and practices. When we make these inclusive tools and mindset part of our default approach to networking, more people will be able to engage with us and our content—and our network will benefit.

Many platforms, such as Squarespace, Wix, Facebook, Instagram, and YouTube, have built-in accessibility tools and user guides, and I've also included some starter resources in appendix B. Easy first steps include making your content more accessible to screen readers (assistive technology/software that helps blind and low-vision readers use digital content) by doing things like tagging photos and videos with alt text, providing captioning for audio resources/videos, and using camel case in hashtags (#NetworkingForIndieWriters rather than #networkingforindiewriters).

> *What is Digital Accessibility? It's enabling people with a disability to experience web-based services, content and other digital products with the same successful outcome as those without disabilities.*
>
> —TYLER M. CAREY, WESTCHESTER PUBLISHING SERVICES

In addition to improving accessibility, these minor adjustments also make your business communications more effective and useful to your audience. For example, using alt text[4] has definite SEO benefits. These short, descriptive phrases allow search engines to access visual content that they would otherwise not have access to (for instance, the JPG of that cool infographic you created). You can also link to a text-based version of informative visual graphics, which aids SEO and allows screen readers to access the actual content.

In addition, when you design images or decide on your brand colors, pay attention to color contrast and how it affects readability for people with color blindness. Likewise, some fonts are more accessible for readers with dyslexia. Be mindful of how your default choices might make it easier or harder for you to connect with potential clients and colleagues online.

It may seem like there's a lot to learn if you want to make your content and communications accessible, but don't get so overwhelmed that you don't even try. Creating accessible content is within your power. Check out the resources in appendix B to get started, and if you can't tackle this now, mark a time in your calendar in the near future when you can.

---

4   Alt text is a short-written piece of text that's associated with a digital image, but hidden, that provides a description of the image for people with visual disabilities.

Writer Check-In:

After completing the website self-assessment worksheet, Adie realized that her website screamed "fangirl," not "professional writer who can get a novel ready for prime time." Here are the top-level changes Adie decided to implement to get her website working for her as part of her networking strategy.

Adie's Action Items for Website:

1. Tone down the neon color scheme; study mystery genre covers and adopt similar colors and fonts as those books on my website.

2. Rewrite my website copy to focus on my readers' or clients' interests/needs.

3. List professional memberships to build credibility.

4. Curate blog content to be more targeted and helpful to my ideal audience.

Quarterly Networking Worksheet

Action Items for My Website:

_____

_____

_____

_____

_____

_____

_____

_____

_____

_____

CHAPTER 6

NETWORKING TACTIC #2
PERSONAL COMMUNICATIONS

It's up to you to create the opportunities for finding connections.

—Michelle Tillis Lederman, The 11 Laws of Likability

It's easy to underestimate the impact that our daily personal communications have on our networking efforts. When we think about a networking plan, we tend to envision a radical commitment to a new way of putting ourselves out there. Something challenging, maybe a little scary—definitely outside our comfort zone. But a happy fact is that networking starts with something as small as how we interact with each person we come into contact with—and we have the power to build our network with something as simple as each email we send.

Were you expecting a herculean task? Is this too easy to be worthwhile? Keep in mind, it will take discipline and thoughtfulness—being aware and in the moment when you might prefer to just phone it in. Relationships are built bit by bit, and when we focus on our communications as an intentional networking tactic, we can leverage the power of incremental growth.

In this context, what counts as "communications"? Our focus will be on email because it's one of the activities most of us have to do every day, but other examples include social media posts, commenting on group platforms—even something as straightforward as an invoice or an out-of-office message. (I like to show my personality with my out-of-office messages. Instead of a disappointing, bland notice that I'm unavailable, many times my messages feature an illustration of an idyllic scene where I say that I'm busy recharging my batteries and will be back energized and better than ever soon. That or some self-deprecating, humorous message about how it's not really a true vacation if I'm bound to spend all this time with my family.)

So, how do we make everyday emails work for us from a networking perspective? Admittedly, this is, in many respects, a less targeted networking tactic than crafting a website, but by paying attention to how we interact with others on a fundamental level, we can develop good communication habits that will make us more successful at cultivating relationships. Let's consider how the message and the medium of our personal communications can contribute to building the network we need.

THE MESSAGE

Networking gets results when we are real and do our best work—when we show that we are easy to work with, conscientious, and professional. We all have bad days, but in networking, we want to build up a picture of who we are on our best days: someone people want to hire, someone people want to hear more from, someone people want to read or trust with their ideas, their project, their image, or their brand. Someone they trust!

So, it's important to be mindful of how we present ourselves and where we focus our energy. We might not always have the wherewithal to be upbeat and personable at the end of a long day, but we'll take the extra five seconds to type out the name of the person we're communicating with—and to close with a "thank you"—rather than firing off a one-liner. There's another person on the receiving end, and they've had a long day too, so take the opportunity to connect with them, even if it's just acknowledging that they're more than just a dispenser of needed information.

Remember that part of building networking relationships is creating room for positive interaction. This means being approachable, showing that we're open to helping others when we can and are interested in their work and challenges.

In the years since the first networking book came out, I've regularly been approached by new (and established) writers who are looking for writing guidance or self-publishing advice. Like many of my peers, I know what it's like to desperately need a word of assurance or the kind of perspective that only comes with years of experience. And because other writers took the time to answer my questions when I was starting out or working through challenges, I make the effort to do the same.

Does this lead to new business? Sometimes it does. Sometimes it doesn't. But networking is about more than increasing the bottom line. It's about building connections that enrich the individual and the group. It's about being open to possibilities and the serendipity that awaits.

Our takeaway: be present, be yourself, and share your strengths.

Communication Tips

- ✉ Regularly check in on readers, or clients and colleagues (congratulate them on successes, wish them a happy birthday, share articles, share your blog post, ask about their project's progress, etc.). Remember to leverage the incremental strength of frequent communication.

- ✉ Don't wait for special occasions—text, post, or email them whenever they're on your mind.

- ✉ You can also set yourself reminders if you often get too caught up in your deadlines to be spontaneous.

- ✉ Don't reach out only when you need something. Everyone wants to be appreciated for who they are, not just what they can do for you.

- ✉ Consider creating a newsletter to give your readers a chance to know you better.

- ✉ Keep track of multicultural holidays so you can be mindful of colleagues' schedules and show respect for their time out of the office.

- ✉ Empty your voicemails regularly. Make sure it's easy for people to communicate with you.

- ✉ Invest in stationery and stamps—send notes!

- ✉ Acknowledge kindnesses with thank-you gifts when appropriate.

Everyday Communications That Need to Align with Your Networking Efforts

- 👤 Your voicemail message (Let your personality come through; be professional but engaging.)

- 👤 Your profile in professional directories (Present a consistent message/brand.)

- 👤 Updates posted on your LinkedIn profile (or the headline you use on LinkedIn)

- 👤 Your headshot on a social media profile

- 👤 Your bio as a speaker, award recipient, or board appointee

- 👤 Your invoice, if you use one (Remember to thank your clients; remind them that referrals are appreciated.)

- 👤 How you participate in a Facebook, Circle, Vox, or Slack space chat

- 👤 Your #IndieAuthor or #AmWriting posts

- 👤 The contact page on your website (Let visitors know your work hours and whether you reply within twenty-four hours/one business day, or another time frame. Set expectations and honor them.)

How you present yourself in any of these "networking encounters" is as important as a VIP invitation, a solid handshake, or an engaging elevator pitch.

THE MEDIUM

I often wish that there were a how-to-exist-in-a-business-environment manual that everyone received at the start of their career. It would tell you things like "be prepared to take ownership of solutions you suggest" and "learn the art of workplace triage." And a whole chapter would be devoted to email best practices, from using executive summaries to the benefits of bullet points to asking direct questions and indicating next steps.

For now, here's a list of some things to keep in mind when crafting effective emails that will show you as the drama-free writer that you are. I've found that implementing these steps contributes to establishing trust with peers and clients, which makes it more likely that we can effectively network with them.

- Create email templates that you can customize. By preparing a thoughtful, helpful response to common requests ahead of time, you'll have more time to focus on engaging with your reader (by adding a personal greeting) and you'll sound less harried, abrupt, or curt. This is also a good tool to prevent the last-minute misspellings that crop up when we're in a hurry. (Note, text expanders are a great tool for this!)

- Make sure to create a vacation response if you're going away for a few days; it lets your client or readers know your absence is planned and that you'll reach them when you return to your office. (Remember, for internet safety, you don't need to say where you're going or with who, just that you won't be able to promptly reply. And if you'd like to learn more about internet safety from a writer's experience, see Judy Mohr's book *Hidden Traps of the Internet: Building and Protecting Your Online Platform*.)

- Create a well-thought-out signature line. Maybe add your social media links or organizations you belong to (which enhances credibility). Or add a quote—whether it's your tagline or your favorite literary one-liner.

- Keep your reader's needs in mind when crafting emails:
  - Use a proper greeting. Take time to acknowledge the person at the other end; balance to-the-point emails with a friendly, welcoming attitude.
  - Acknowledge and appreciate your reader's efforts or contributions to date.
  - State the purpose of the email. Keep it to the point and focus on the details that are necessary for decision-making.
  - Use bullet points or other formatting techniques to keep important information or questions from being lost in the main text.
  - Ask direct questions.
  - Recap your understanding of the situation or the next steps. Be clear about dates and deadlines. Setting expectations is key.
  - Offer to answer questions (or even talk on the phone).
  - Thank your reader.

Self-Assessment Worksheet: Communication Habits

General

What are your preferred communication methods (phone calls, text, email, etc.)?

_____

Does your preferred method align with your clientsí and colleaguesí preferences?

_____

If not, what adjustments can you make to increase your comfort level while accommodating their needs?

_____

_____

What communication habits of others do you find most frustrating (running counter to clear communication)?

_____

_____

Which of your own habits might hinder clear communication and relationship building?

_____

_____

Email evaluation

Do you routinely include an addressee line (ìDear Ana,î ìHi, Joyî)?   Yes   No

Do you include a personal greeting?   Yes   No

How do you sign off?_____

   Do you invite further discussion or signal your availability to answer questions?

_____

   Are your website and social media links included in your signature?   Yes   No

   Is a business tagline included in your signature?   Yes   No

Are the main professional organizations you're a member of included in your signature?   Yes   No

Are your messages long and detailed?   Yes   No

Are they as short as humanly possible?   Yes   No

Do you use bullet points to highlight specific questions needing answers?   Yes   No

Describe the general tone of your communications in three words: _____

_____

Now, randomly select five emails from your Sent box (no more than a month old).

Do your answers in the previous section match up with what you find in the actual emails? _____

Note the differences and evaluate whether adjusting your communication style might avoid misunderstandings, improve efficiency, engage your reader, encourage finding solutions, or create space for getting to know others and allowing yourself to be known as a person behind the writing.

_____

_____

_____

Select a few emails from two of your contacts whose emails are consistently clear, actionable—and personable.

Apply the email evaluation questions to their emails and note the answers.

What takeaways can you apply to your own communication style? _____

_____

_____

_____

_____

BONUS!

Things That Make Networking Easier

- A short, to-the-point pitch

- Email templates (for praise, for introductions, for rejecting work, for referring work, for thank-yous, for sharing resources)

- Testimonials on website or printed material

- Business cards

- Updated LinkedIn profile with most current work projects

- Clickable contact information on everything that represents you (email signature, contracts, proposals)

- Asking for referrals/reviews on your invoice

- Samples of your work

A WRITER'S PERSPECTIVE

As an author you need to network—if for no other reason—for the sake of your own mental health. By obvious necessity, writing is a solitary and isolating act. Nobody prepares you for the weight of upkeeping an entire world and untangling its infinite plots in the back of your mind at all times, nor for the sole responsibility of getting that world out into people's hands. So find people who are at the same stage as you and scream into the void together. Find people who are a few steps ahead of you to prepare for what's coming. Find people a few steps behind you to warn them of the folly of the path they've set down upon. Because nobody outside of this world—not your partner, not your parents, and not your friends—can really understand. Trust me: find some other writers or you'll go mad (and not in the fun, productive kind of way).

—**NATHAN MAKARYK,** AUTHOR OF *Nottingham and Lionhearts*

INSIGHT: THE IMPORTANCE OF BEING... YOURSELF

Because networking is often spoken of as this critical but elusive magical elixir that we must obtain in order to succeed, many of us let that pressure spill over into our networking efforts. We expect instant networking results and sometimes treat others like networking PEZ dispensers. We feel the need to be "on" all the time, to turn everyday encounters into hard sales pitches, or to squeeze the life out of every opportunity even when we would make a much better impression—and lay the groundwork for a real relationship—if we just took a breath and respected others' boundaries. The result of this networking pressure is that we sometimes come across as being rather self-centered, even if that's not our intention.

At the same time, some of us feel the need to self-censor, to strip our communications of personality so that we can fit in as "professional." The result is that we're uncomfortable, and we end up sounding flat or fake. At the very least, we just blend into the background. It's something others pick up on almost subconsciously, and it's a surefire way to sabotage our networking efforts.

None of this should come as a surprise—when we're under pressure, it's a natural reaction to want to doggedly push forward or, conversely, to stay safe inside the time-honored lines. This competing sensation is the networking version of "fight, freeze, or flight."

Instead, try to settle in—into being yourself.

We each have our own voice, which comes through in our speech, writing, and expressive choices—from our brand colors to our preferred fonts. That unique voice is an essential part of our networking—it's our signature. When we allow ourselves to be *ourselves*, to embrace our quirks and idiosyncrasies while still being hardworking, skilled practitioners of our chosen vocations, that's when we become, as writer and editor Louise Harnby says, "interesting" and "memorable." That's when we feel comfortable in our own skin, when we have confidence in our abilities, and when we can make the real connections that networks are built on. Superficial networks don't create nurturing communities and don't bring the leads and opportunities that we're looking for. To build deep, effective, multilayered networks, we have to be—as clichéd as it may sound—true to ourselves. And in doing so, we can create networks that are inclusive, supportive, and enriching.

> *A network doesn't just have to be who you meet at work, but rather anyone in your 360-degree purview.*
>
> —SAMANTHA NOLAN, NOLAN BRANDING

Writer Check-In:

After Adie reviewed her own email habits, she realized that in her attempt to sound professional, she was in robot-writer mode (a.k.a. AI mode) way too much—and it was keeping her relationships on a superficial level. Adie chose four simple steps to help position her personal communications for more effective networking.

Adie's Action Items for Personal Communications:

1. Take the time to say hello and connect on a human-to-human basis.

2. Create a complete email signature with my contact information and a link to where they can connect with me on social media.

3. Make sure to respond to emails within 24 hours.

4. Say "thank you" more.

Quarterly Networking Worksheet

Action Items for My Personal Communications:

_____

_____

_____

_____

_____

_____

_____

_____

_____

_____

CHAPTER 7

NETWORKING TACTIC #3
SOCIAL MEDIA

My top platform for ongoing networking is Facebook groups. They're free to use; can welcome you 24/7 regardless of geographical location; can be broad or structured around a person or a topic; most professional organizations have one; it offers a range of privacy settings to suit members' requirements, and provide a space for shy persons in which to lurk and learn without feeling uncomfortable.

—LOUISE HARNBY, FICTION WRITER, EDITOR, & PROOFREADER

In today's overwhelming world, where media follows us everywhere and we're expected to be actively engaging with our clients, potential clients, and colleagues—all while performing on social media platforms, saying something interesting and useful—networking can seem especially stressful. How do we keep up with trends? With technology? Who should we really connect with? Which is the right platform to post what kind of information? Do we need to be on all of them? Will our private lives be revealed? So many valid questions!

Most of us started off on social media as a way to stay in touch with friends and family who live far away. It's been years since social media has evolved from just that (and not always in a positive way), but today we know through some hard data that being on social media is another important way to connect with clients and readers (among an extensive list of other benefits and perils).

Whatever your beliefs are about social media, I want to encourage you to think of it as a tool in your kit that can bring great rewards if used correctly and in a manner that works for *you*. If you're social media averse (and many writers are), you can go ahead and hop over to chapter 8 ... or consider staying with me to explore whether there are some fun, low-stress ways to make social media part of your networking strategy.

Forbes Insights published a study titled "Business Meetings: The Case for Face-to-Face," which discussed the perceived value of in-person meetings and networking versus virtual activities. Though many people preferred in-person interactions, others reported some distinct advantages of virtual engagement:

- Saves time (92 percent)
- Saves money (88 percent)
- More flexibility in location and timing (76 percent)
- Allows the participant to multitask (64 percent)
- Increases productivity (55 percent)
- Ability to archive sessions (49 percent)
- Less peer pressure (16 percent)

Interesting way to look at our social media time, right?

So, let's assess your current social media presence with the following exercise.

Self-Assessment Worksheet: Social Media Checkup

Which platforms do you have an account with?

_____

_____

Which platforms do you use on a weekly basis?

_____

_____

On which platform do you regularly engage with others?

_____

_____

Which is your favorite platform? _____

Which is your least favorite?_____

How do these platforms align with the platforms your desired network members use most (revisit chapter 4, if needed)? _____

_____

For each platform you're on, ask:

Are you successful? _____

How do you define that success (number of followers/meaningful engagements/ job opportunities/feeling in the know/learning new things/forming relationships)?

_____

_____

Are you measuring your efforts and results—or just going by feel?

_____

_____

CHOOSING A PLATFORM

We don't have all the time in the world to be on social media, so it's crucial to choose one or two platforms that we can work with—and that we actually enjoy using. Yes, *enjoy*!

Even if you avoid social media, you undoubtedly know the major platforms that are out there, you know which ones you've tried (successfully or unsuccessfully), and you probably know which you should consider using—in terms of both your target audience and your own comfort level. If you're not sure, try the short quiz by Interact called "What Social Media Platform Is Best for You?" Though it's not a one-stop solution to choosing a platform, it will give you a pretty good idea of where you should start based on your goals and your target client and reader demographics.

Before we continue, a word about "The Best Social Media Platform for Networking": Let's dispel the myth right now. There is no *best* social media platform for networking. They can all be great—or time-sucking nightmares—depending on how you use them. Every successful writer I know uses or swears by different social media platforms. There are the unwavering Instagram fans. The Facebook devotees who only follow Facebook writing groups. Or those who connect on TikTok. What matters is what comes naturally to you, what you are interested in or willing to devote a bit of time to, and ultimately, where you can connect with your desired network members. Don't let anyone convince you one is better than the others. You might find a fit and be successful right from the start, or like me, it may take testing different waters to discover which platform you enjoy the most.

With that in mind, using the insights from chapter 4 about who you want to connect with, let's find out where your ideal clients and colleagues are spending time online. Start by asking your former or existing clients what social media they use. Ask fellow indie authors which platform works best for their social media strategy. If you don't know any authors yet, check out the organizations I list in appendix A, or the Facebook writing groups, and find authors who share your specialty. Where do these potential networking contacts spend time online?

Talking with your network about their social media strategy may also open the door to a deeper discussion, allowing you to discover opportunities to help your colleagues and clients as well. But even if you're not ready to talk with peers and clients about their social media, you can easily research where they are online and evaluate their content and engagement. When you know where they're most active, you can use that information to guide your own social media strategy.

Next, to add another layer of depth to this research, consider lurking on writer or self-publishing discussion lists, forums, and message boards. Search for keywords that reflect your area of expertise (e.g., "academic writer," "translator," "ghostwriter," "copywriter," "content creator," etc.). You get the idea! Do that same type of keyword search on Google, LinkedIn, or Medium. Focus on the platforms you enjoy using to understand what's happening there regarding these industry-specific topics. Combine this with what you learned by talking with clients and peers, then complete either the form below or the social media–overlap diagram on the next page (or both!) so that it's very clear where *you* need to be.

Let's see what you've discovered so far.

Which social media platforms are my desired network contacts using?

Readers or clients: _____

_____

_____

_____

_____

_____

Peers: _____

_____

_____

_____

_____

_____

Which social media platform(s) are comfortable for me now? _____

_____

_____

_____

Where is the overlap? _____

_____

_____

_____

_____

_____

_____

_____

The Social Media Overlap

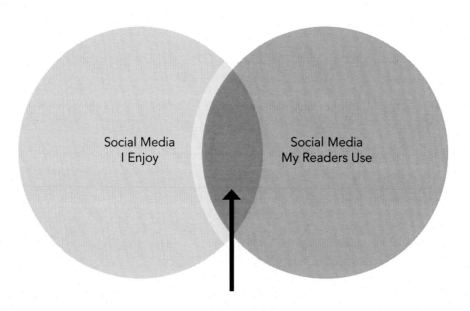

Social Media
I Enjoy

Social Media
My Readers Use

Where We Meet
(and They Find Me!)

Social media–overlap diagram.

If there is overlap, then great! You know which platform(s) to focus your efforts on for this quarter. If not, then dig a bit deeper. Ask yourself, *Why is this particular social media comfortable for me?* Then ask, *How can I use this knowledge to help me succeed with the platform that my desired network is most active on?*

For example, our indie writer colleague Alejandro might be comfortable with using Facebook because he's been on it for years, but Facebook is overwhelming and chaotic to him. However, many of his target clients and fellow writing professionals are most active on Facebook. How can he make Facebook feel more personal and focus his circle of engagement there? One answer is to use lists to craft a more custom Facebook experience. By being open to examining his comfort zone and learning about his discomfort zone, Alejandro can create a compromise that will enable him to network more effectively with the people he most needs to reach.

This analysis of where your clients and peers are spending time online is something you should consider doing once a year—after you've set your business goals. This information is going to change over time, so what you write today will be different a few years from now, and that's how it should be. Some platforms will fall out of favor, and new ones will emerge. (This is one reason to make sure you have an online space you control: your website.)

Once you've worked through the preceding exercises and completed your research, you should have a solid idea of where your clients and peers are active online and which platform(s) you're willing to try. Now choose one to two platforms to focus and practice on for the next three months. I suggest a minimum of three months so that you have the chance to see tangible results and measure whether what you're doing is paying off. (How much time are you spending on social media? Are you forming relationships? Are you learning about your clients' needs? Are you building your brand?)

LINDA RUGGERI'S PERSPECTIVE

I love photography, gardening, baking, and home décor, so I'm naturally drawn to Instagram and Pinterest, which are more visual outlets for creative people. I like some blogs, but I don't have time to read many of them, so I follow very few bloggers, and usually, the blogs I do read are related to writing or editing. I spend very little time on Facebook, and when I do, it's only to post images of book releases or tips for writers and editors (even though there are some amazing groups I belong to and should participate in more). On LinkedIn, I follow a lot of agents and publishers to learn about publishing trends or what the market is looking for. Once or twice a month I will post what I learned about a recent event I might have attended and those posts get a lot of impressions. A few times a week I spend a bit of time on TikTok, but this is a platform I'm still just observing and learning from others.

Since I do spend time on Instagram, I take advantage of what I've learned and enjoy, and I've created an account that's dedicated to book reviews, bookstagrams, and tips for writers (@theinsightfuleditor). A few years ago I took a self-paced class by Sara Tasker that I really enjoyed, which gave me some valuable pointers (Me & Orla). I've also studied the accounts I like and figured out what they have in common, and what I could build on my own page that reflects my brand, my style, my interests, and my work. Then, a lot of these posts get automatically shared on my Facebook author/editor page, and on my Pinterest business account. I've slowly built a small yet organic following (without the help of outside agents), and although the number of followers may not be in the thousands, they are a tight, genuine, and curated group of creatives that I enjoy interacting with.

WHAT TO POST:
CREATING MEANINGFUL CONTENT

Now that you've committed to trying a couple of social media platforms, it's time to decide what to post. As I mentioned earlier, if we're going to spend time (that it often feels like we don't have) on social media to attract clients and build relationships with fellow authors, we need to offer content that adds value. There are no set rules for writers for creating content; most of us discover our message as we go. The key, however, is that our content needs to bring value. I can't stress that enough.

And remember, when on social media, you should always be doing one of these three things:

1. Creating content (protecting it when necessary through copyright)
2. Sharing content
3. Commenting on content

If you maintain a balance between these three aspects of posting online, it ensures that you're contributing to your online community by sharing your own unique insights, curating and promoting quality information, and engaging with others.

Now let's return, for a moment, to our definition of *networking*: behavior that builds a web of mutually beneficial relationships. To get the most from our time on social media, we'll combine our definition of *networking* with our most important posting advice (add value). The result is a philosophy that helps us stay focused in the midst of social media information overload: build relationships by adding value.

As with all the networking tactics, using social media for networking comes down to using what you have (your unique voice and point of view) on the platforms you and your network like to use. The goal isn't to be famous or simply accrue ever more followers, but to reach your target audience (a.k.a. the potential readers or clients who need you and your services, and the peers you can learn from and grow with). As you keep these guidelines in mind, your social media skills will improve and your network will expand to support your business.

Allow yourself to take the time to grow your audience *organically*. Let your followers come to you—as they discover you through your content.

And how do you do that?

By adding *value*.

By giving your peers and future clients information that will bring value to their professional lives. You might offer clients a tool, a word list, an idea, a hard-to-remember style rule, or an inspirational quote. You might share with other writers how you overcame freelancing challenges. The value you bring can be so many different things, but the starting place for knowing what to post is knowing who you're trying to reach and what they need.

Get ready to brainstorm, and write your answers in the space provided.

For Readers or Clients

Who is my ideal reader or client? _____

_____

_____

_____

_____

_____

What do they need? (What problem can I help them solve?) _____

_____

_____

_____

_____

_____

What content can I offer them, based on my expertise? (What solution do I have for their problem?) _____

_____

_____

_____

_____

_____

As we discussed earlier, your fellow industry professionals should also be key players in your network. You'll learn from them, exchange ideas, help them and offer support, receive client referrals from them, and make client referrals to them when a project comes along that's not a good fit for you. Some of these peers you might already know, and some you have yet to meet.

For Peers

Who is my ideal colleague? _____

_____

_____

_____

_____

_____

What do they need? (What problem can I help them solve? How can I support their work?)

_____

_____

_____

_____

_____

What keywords do fellow writers or authors use in their directory profiles and bios?

_____

_____

_____

_____

_____

What topics do they discuss on social media? _____

_____

_____

_____

_____

_____

How can I add to the conversation? (What kind of content/engagement can I contribute?)

_____

_____

_____

_____

_____

INSIGHT: MY SOCIAL MEDIA STRATEGY

Example

I'm a nonfiction writer and editor specializing in memoir, so I create content like:

- outline advice for memoir writers,

- writing tools for nonfiction writers (spell check, Grammarly, books on writing),

- inspirational quotes (to keep writing, to stay with it),

- suggestions of memoir best practices, and

- memoir bookstagrams (curated pictures of memoirs I've read) with reviews (why I liked them and why you should read it).

If I'm posting on Instagram (@theinsightfuleditor), I'll make sure to include relevant hashtags at the end of my post in camel case like,

#NonfictionWriter

#WritingCoach

#WritingCommunity

#WritersLife

#NetworkingForWriters

#WhenImNotWriting and #WhenImNotEditing (my favorites to show that I'm also not a productivity robot).

The hashtags I follow are #Memoir, #MemoirWriter, #Cookbooks, #EscritoresLatinos, #AutoresLatinos, #BookBinding, #BookLovers, and #WomenWriters. When I see posts with these hashtags, I'll look at the ones that interest me, and comment with helpful information or to say something nice about the post or the author of the post. I'm training the algorithm.

Results

Although I seldom get a direct message that turns into a client off of social media (if I do get one it's on LinkedIn), my brand (The Insightful Editor) and I get exposure. I try to feed the algorithm daily with content that's related to my goals, and my followers can learn about my books, where I'm speaking, what workshops I'm leading, as well as get a tiny glimpse into my personal world and the things that bring me joy (baking, gardening, and mom moments). And here's the bit of wisdom: My followers aren't always my clients; however, my followers are the ones that will refer a client to me because it's clear from my posts what work I do.

So who follows me? Creatives of all ages, from all over the world, who are either writers, editors, or book lovers. I'm not looking to make a client or to sell a book to every follower. For me, being on Instagram is easy, fun, and a wonderful creative experience. And if the content I'm creating can inspire or educate a fellow writer or editor, then that's a positive outcome. By looking at my content, you can get a pretty good feel for my personality too.

Keep in mind that when clients come to you because someone else referred them, they'll often decide to vet you by looking at what social media platforms you're active on and what you're posting. Do they share the same interests? Do they feel like they have a sense for who you are? It might just be that one quote/photo/tip that you post that makes someone feel you are the author or writer *for them*. Sometimes, it's the content that creates the credibility your client is looking for.

SOCIAL MEDIA IN ACTION

Maybe your clients could benefit from reading about tips for writing their graduate dissertation, or strengthening a character's story arc in your screenplay, or finding a literary agent or publisher. Maybe they need to know the "Five Must-Do Things for Blog Content Writing." I can't tell you what content you should publish, but I can tell you it has to be relevant to the type of client you're looking to attract. And like all things, it will take time to build an audience. Give yourself three to six months to experiment and see what results you get, and if you don't feel you're gaining traction, you can try something else.

LINDA RUGGERI'S PERSPECTIVE

If you look at my social media feed, you can clearly see year by year how my brand has changed, how my subject matter has evolved. At the beginning it was mostly landscapes, famous quotes by writers, and books. Other years, my content has been more about plants, flowers, butterflies, and books. Then, during the Covid years the posts were about sourdough, baking desserts, and books. We're humans; it's natural that we change, that our interests shift and evolve. Just try to keep a through line in what you post that's related to the type of reader or client you're hoping to attract.

One of the greatest things about social media (and there aren't many) is that any post or comment can be deleted at any time should you make a mistake or change your mind. Don't let the fear of being imperfect stop you from posting. You probably have a writing buddy who can look over your posts when you're just getting started—and you can do the same for them. This is part of being in a trusted network—and all the more reason for you to cultivate your own.

Once you've determined *what* type of content you can offer, it's time to envision *how* you can offer it—in a way that's easy to access and attractive. Using the keywords that identify the type of material you write, search through your chosen platform, and see what kinds of posts are appealing and pique your interest. This isn't so you can copy what someone else is doing. It's to get you thinking about *what you like* and *what you can do*. The content you share should reflect your brand colors (maybe even the same font you use on your website), your voice, and your style. Make the content yours, but be consistent so people can identify your brand and the work you do.

When you look at how others are sharing their content, be analytical. Notice what content is original and what is shared or repurposed content. If you look closely, not everything you post has to be perfect or original. Sometimes sharing someone's post that you appreciate is enough.

My go-to platforms for when I'm looking for value content that won't take me down a rabbit hole are Instagram, LinkedIn, a few websites (Jane

Friedman, Kindlepreneur, Independent Book Publishers Association, Shelf Awareness, Writer's Digest, and The Creative Penn, and sometimes Facebook. Yes, there are many more platforms or websites I could explore where successful writers are showcasing their work, but there is only so much time I want to spend in front of a screen. Other good ones where you might find inspiration are YouTube, TikTok, Reddit, Wattpad, Bluesky, Substack, Telegram, and Discord... but also, your local bookstore and your local library!

Facebook

- Ask a Book Editor
- The Aspiring Travel Writer
- Author Nation (formerly 20 Books to 50k)
- Blogging Boost
- Fantasy Author Collective
- The Freelance Content Marketing Writer
- Indie Author Group
- The Indiepreneur Writers Collective
- Indie Writers Unite!
- NanoLand (based on NaNoWriMo)
- Successful Indie Author
- Word Nerds Unite
- The Write Life Community
- Writers Helping Writers
- Writers Write
- Writing Bad
- The Writing Gals

LinkedIn

- Ashley Alvarado (journalist, writer)
- Ben Riggs (writer, editor, communications specialist)
- Carol Tice (author, ghostwriter)
- Dennis Williams II (content marketing manager)
- Kevin Cokley (psychology professor and writer)
- Mandalit del Barco (news reporter)
- Michael Spencer (freelance copywriter)
- Michelle Lowery (digital content editor)
- Mukti Masih (content writer, brand storywriter)
- Sophie Michals (technical writer)
- Stephanie Jentz (story writer, podcasts)
- Suzy Bills (writer, editor, instructor)

Instagram

@angiethomas (Angie Thomas, MG, YA, author of *Nic Blake and the Remarkables*)

@btleditorial (Hannah Bauman, editor, author, and writing coach)

@cardinalrulepress (indie publisher, inclusive books for kids)

@chimamanda_adichie (Chimamanda Adichie, author of *Notes on Grief*)

@janefriedman (Jane Friedman, author of *The Business of Being a Writer*)

@karensoffice (Karen Yin, author of *The Conscious Style Guide*)

@krakauernotwriting (Jon Krakauer, writer, author of *Into the Wild*)

@me_and_orla (Sara Tasker, Instagram expert, writer, author of *Hashtag Authentic*)

@mixtusmedia (Jenn dePaula, book marketer)

Pinterest

Aerogramme Writers' Studio (writing resources)

Heidi Fiedler (creative and writing resources)

Jody Hedlund (best-selling author)

Kellie Coates Gilbert (author, women's fiction)

Lucinda Brant (indie author)

Sylvia Day (*New York Times* best-selling author)

Writer's Relief (writing resources)

> *Thirty-five percent of survey participants said a casual conversation through LinkedIn Messaging led to a new opportunity.*
>
> —LinkedIn Corporate Communications

Other Ways to Gain Organic Followers

Another way of making yourself and your services known is by mindfully commenting on other people's posts. The key word here is *mindfully*. You don't want to come out and blatantly state that you're a writer they can hire for their dissertation or manuscript, or, worse yet, correct their grammar publicly. (Everyone despises the grammar police! UK editor Denise Cowle addresses this in her article "Why the Grammar Police Aren't Cool.") Instead, you want to think of how to encourage writers with their work and offer some insight, whether by suggesting a book to read or sharing a piece of wisdom that helped you overcome a writing challenge.

Blogging (or even writing mini blogs if you're tight on time) is still another great way to drive organic social media growth. For example, if your platform of choice is LinkedIn, the options for networking are endless. Initially, most of us used this platform as a place to create our résumés and look for jobs. However, nowadays LinkedIn has become so much more than that, and if you use it wisely, you can reap a lot of benefits from it.

So, if you don't have a website or blog where you can post your ideas, do it on LinkedIn by creating a LinkedIn article, which is basically a blog post that's written right there on your LinkedIn home page (it's a small orange icon at the bottom right of the "Start a post" window).

If you'd like to create an article (for example, "Five Tips to Be a Great Mystery Writer"), make sure to include a background image, use keywords (to improve your SEO), and include at least one hyperlink (where the reader can find more information). Make your articles short, sweet, and meaningful. For information on how to do this effectively, you can check out "Publish Articles on LinkedIn."

Remember, the key is to share information your target audience is interested in, while showing your personality and interests.

SCHEDULE YOUR CONTENT

It took me a long time to decide to do this, but the most effective and efficient way for me to post on social media is when I plan what I want to say a week in advance, and schedule the posts ahead of time. My feed is about 70% planned content and 30% spontaneous content.

What works for me is to pick one day out of the week and set aside an hour to *plan* my posts and gather what I need for them (I do this usually on Sundays, or Monday mornings). I keep a social media folder, with subfolders, with the content I need to create my posts. This helps me have a place to drop things into during the week, and then just copy and paste what I need when I'm ready to schedule. This way I'm not duplicating content either. I also use a caption template with pre-existing hashtags that I can edit as needed when I post. My scheduler of preference right now is Meta Business Suite (via Facebook) because it's free and meets my small business goals.

This is what my social media folder structure looks like:

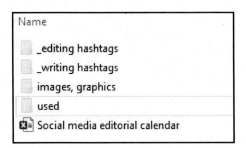

Name

_editing hashtags
_writing hashtags
images, graphics
used
Social media editorial calendar

If you keep telling yourself you don't have time to promote your writing on social media, here are a few tips that might make the experience more productive:

- You don't always have to be creating new content. Stick to simple, manageable tasks (e.g., "Monday: comment on five posts").

- Stick to attainable goals (e.g., "Wednesday: one original content post on LinkedIn").

- Find non-time-consuming posts (e.g., "Friday: share someone else's content with a short comment on FB"). This is one of the easiest ways to participate—instead of lurk—on social media and a great way to gain new followers. If you are going to comment on a book, try to focus on the positive, and what worked for you. If you have something negative to say, I'm an advocate of the "sandwich" approach.

- Make your social media accessible. Most social media apps have desktop versions that are easier to use (especially if you have to type!).

- Download all your social media posts to your desktop and keep a folder with the content you post as a backup. Remember, you can repurpose that content again later in the year or next year. And more importantly, if someone hacks into your account, you have those posts saved and can repost them (yes, this does happen).

- Consider using a social media scheduling platform like Hootsuite, Later, Buffer, Meta Business Suite, etc.

There is this rule that many people active on social media follow called the "30/30/30 rule." Although interpretations of it vary slightly, the one I feel helps us the most is by marketing strategist Paulette Duderstadt on LinkedIn:

> *30 percent of the time—be A LEADER in your industry on social.... Post about trends, business challenges and business outcomes, and information that is simply forward-thinking.*

> *30 percent of the time—be A CHEERLEADER for your industry.... Too often [we] are laser-focused on posting all about the business. It's not all us, us, us in the business world.*

> *30 percent of the time—be an ADVOCATE or AMBASSADOR for your community. Community means your employees, your clients, your neighborhood, and everything that you are passionate about. It may be raising awareness for an important fundraising event like a 10k walk that is aimed to do good.*

> *So what happened to the other 10 percent? SHARE, SHARE, and SHARE. Sharing or liking or even commenting on social posts expands your reach and says that you are paying attention. So share what's important to your business and to you.*

EXPANDING YOUR NETWORK

Here are a few more points for good networking etiquette while on social media. Check off the ones you are already doing:

- ☐ Follow people you look up to.

- ☐ Follow clients you enjoy working with (to learn about their business, their interests).

- ☐ Follow potential clients you'd like to work with (to learn about their business, their interests).

- ☐ Follow colleagues you respect (to learn about new business opportunities, classes, or trends).

- ☐ Comment mindfully and genuinely (avoid a standard comment that gets pasted everywhere, and avoid using only emoji unless you know the person personally and have that type of rapport).

- ☐ Don't follow people expecting them to follow you back.

- ☐ Don't follow people only to unfollow them later; in other words, don't follow someone just to get them to follow you back, and then unfollow them as soon as they do.

- ☐ Be mindful about commenting on controversial topics (politics, religion). It's important to be true to your convictions, but as a businessperson, be aware that the line between "personal" and "professional" is tenuous. Make sure you're prepared for the potential consequences of your words.

- ☐ Avoid social media if you are angry or upset, and never use it for venting about a client.

- ☐ If you want the algorithm to recommend your account to others, or to get the type of content you enjoy, you need to *train* it. Your feed is made up of the content you tend to follow.

- ☐ Enjoy it and have fun!

A WRITER'S PERSPECTIVE

By joining two online marketing groups the year prior to my book's publication date, I was able to connect with other authors who also had books coming out that same year. Both were diverse groups of about thirty people each. The groups provided support with pre-pub, launches, and post-pub. Beyond sharing celebratory moments and frustrations, we advocated one another's books across social media platforms. It's been three years since my first book's publication and our groups continue with an ebb and flow of authors. It's important to give more than you ask; supporting other authors brings you more wholly into the community and grows your online presence and reach—plus you make some great friends along the way!

—**CHRISTINE VAN ZANDT,** AUTHOR OF *Milkweed for Monarchs*
AND *A Brief History of Underpants*

Writer Check-In:

Analyzing her social media presence revealed to Adie that she's been using LinkedIn a lot, which is great for connecting with other publishing professionals, but she's been avoiding TikTok, which is where a lot of indie authors are active. So, she's decided to get out of her comfort zone and research how other indie authors are using TikTok, and then she'll create a plan that blends what she's learned with her current comfort zone. She knows it doesn't have to be perfect, and that she can delete posts if she's not getting the results she needs. But, at the end of three months, she will have expanded her social media reach and—she hopes—her comfort zone.

Adie's Action Items for Social Media:

1. Research colleagues who specialize in indie genre fiction and make note of which platforms they use—and how they engage with the clients and each other.

2. Visit TikTok and search for writers, find a few I like and note

    a. What content (subject matter) are they posting?

    b.   Are they using images or videos? With music? With captions? How long are the videos?

    c.   How long are the post descriptions? How many hashtags? What hashtags?

3.   Based on discoveries, create a weekly plan for the two platforms I want to focus on for the next three months.

Quarterly Networking Worksheet

Action Items for My Social Media:

_____

_____

_____

_____

_____

_____

_____

_____

_____

CHAPTER 8

NETWORKING TACTIC #4
PROFESSIONAL GROUPS

> *Make your network a source of joy. Build one full of people who you enjoy spending time with and helping. Who care about your development and success and with who you're comfortable revealing your setbacks and seeking their counsel.*

> —MARIE KONDO AND SCOTT SONENSHEIN, JOY AT WORK

Being part of a professional organization is an excellent way to stay informed of trends, events, or news that could affect your business (both positively and negatively, like when California Assembly Bill 5 came out). Membership also provides access to vetted classes and continuing education opportunities. Some professional groups I encourage you to check out are the Alliance of Independent Authors, the American Booksellers Association, Sisters in Crime, Romance Writers of America, the American Society of Professional Copywriters, the American Medical Writers Association, and so many more. Appendix A has a more extensive list of writing- and publishing-related organizations.

Just remember—it's not about joining a bunch of groups (it will become overwhelming if you do). Instead, **focus on the top one or two that resonate most** with you now and promise the information and support that will move you closer to your goals. (As your career progresses, it's okay to drop memberships that are no longer relevant to the type of work you want to do. You can always go back to them later if you feel they would add value to your business.)

An effective way of determining which groups to join is to check in with your goals (the immediate and long-term ones) and use them as a guide to decide which groups might be a good fit. You can ponder questions like the following:

- Which groups can help you reach and meet potential clients you can network with?

- Which groups have professional directories or job boards?

- Which groups market to potential clients on behalf of the membership?

- Which groups have conferences, live webinars, or meetups that will teach you something new, while providing opportunities to meet clients or readers?

- Which groups attend the specialty conferences that your target readers attend?

If your goal is to move into a new niche or genre and you need to sharpen or acquire new writing skills or tools, there are other questions to consider:

- Which groups offer educational webinars, classes, chapter meetings, or discussion lists?

- Which groups provide volunteer opportunities?

- Which groups support the trade publications in your niche?

- Which colleagues are in the know regarding industry trends, resources, and tools? What organizations do they belong to?

Once you've found an organization you're interested in, visit its "Resources" page.

- What type of information and resources does it offer its members?

- Does it have a membership directory where you can be listed? Can potential clients find you there?

- Does it have an online forum where members exchange ideas, tips, resources, and maybe even job referrals?

- Does it have a local chapter you can join (whether online or in person)?

- Does the website have an open job board or a job list?

- Does it have volunteer opportunities for members?

- What other membership benefits does it offer? (For example, does it have curated newsletters, discounts on software or insurance, free classes or publications, a mentorship program, or publishing opportunities?)

- How tech savvy is the organization? Does it have a professional, easy-to-navigate website?

- How much are the dues, and are there student rates or scholarships?

- Do current members encourage you to join—or recommend other organizations instead?

To help you decide which group(s) to join, use the following professional-organization comparison tool on the next page. The first line has an example to get you started. Because there are so many good groups, but we all have limited funds (and time), using a tool like this can help us evaluate which groups are most promising at this point in our careers.

 Before joining an organization, ask members about their experiences in the group; sign up for a trial period or lurk a bit if possible before committing to an annual membership.

Self-Assessment Worksheet:
Professional-Organization Comparison Tool

Organization	Location	Membership Cost	Targeted Toward	Has Educational Programs	Has Discussion List/Forum
Society of Children's Book Writers and Illustrators (SCBWI)	US	$100	children's book writers	yes	yes
Total Cost		$100			

Has Online Directory	Other Benefits	My Interest Level	Results	Renew
yes	mentorship program, discounts to conferences	high	Was found by one client in first month. Received referral from fellow member that turned into work.	yes

INSIGHT: NETWORKING IN PERSON

Networking virtually seems to have become the default since the pandemic. For many people it's been beneficial to be able to do this from the comfort of one's own home, and those with accessibility requirements have felt more of a sense of inclusion. For others, however, the in-person social connections have made us feel engaged and present, we've been reminded what it feels like to be face to face with smiles or laughter from a colleague, we've benefitted from the spontaneity of decisions made in the moment (*Want to grab a bite to eat?*), and our bodies have remembered what it's like to react to another person's body language. A Forbes study by contributor Roger Dooley stated that in virtual meetings forty-two percent of call participants don't have their camera on. As someone who has given many networking presentations before, and is always looking to learn more from the audience, I can't tell you how disappointing this is. How am I expected to remember you and what you do if I can't see you? As humans, we communicate in both verbal and nonverbal ways.

A WRITER'S PERSPECTIVE

When I call myself a full-time writer, that isn't a narrow, exclusive term. I'm a Middle-Grade author, a journalist, an editor, and a ghostwriter. Even though the audiences and clients are different, the way I network is the same. People are people, and they all crave a connection and rapport, which builds trust, loyalty, and a desire to want to work with that person. In-person events are the best because something magical, or perhaps biological, happens when you are in the physical presence of another human being. Eye contact, an intimate environment, and casual conversation are my bread and butter. Breaking bread with someone or having a drink with them, even if it's simply a coffee, allows for connection. I don't ever sell my services in those situations. Instead, I allow space for a natural bond to form through story-sharing and laughter, after which most people will desire to continue the conversation and look for ways to work with me. It is a very natural, organic process, but one that doesn't happen as easily unless you are in the person's physical presence. You have to get out there in the world, shake hands, buy someone a drink, and hand them your card. To me, there is no better way to network and no better way to do business.

—JOHN PERAGINE, MANAGING EDITOR AT WORLD CHANGING BOOKS AND AUTHOR OF *Max and the Spice Thieves* SERIES

Rethink Going National

While the national and international conferences get all the glory, they can also be challenging because of the cost of travel and lodging, not to mention the conference registration fee and time out of our work schedules. A few ways to make it more affordable include 1) volunteering to staff the registration check-in (some organizations give volunteers free or discounted admission), 2) sharing lodging (which is also a great way to have a guaranteed conference buddy), and 3) planning your vacation to follow the conference (for example, if you have to go to Denver for business, use it as a jumping-off point for sightseeing in the West).

Go Local

Check out local and regional conferences and events. The costs may be more feasible if you can drive instead of fly, and you might be able to reduce your lodging costs by having fewer nights away from home. From a networking perspective, another advantage of attending local meetings and conferences is that often they are smaller and provide the chance to get to know people better. If you don't love large gatherings, these small meetings can be less stressful and provide easier opportunities to socialize. And because these events tend to draw from the surrounding area, there's a good chance that you'll be able to keep up the in-person contact with the friends you make. Good opportunities are full-day workshops, a weekend writing retreat, or an extension class at a local university, community college, or library.

Be Kind to Yourself

Some of us are extroverted, and for some of us, it's an effort to feel at ease in an unfamiliar social setting. In either case, there are things we can do to get the most out of networking at conferences. One approach is self-care: pay attention to your nutrition, safeguard your sleep, and find ways to give yourself the needed quiet time even in the face of the excitement and distractions of the conference. Another idea is to make plans to network and socialize while you're still at home in your comfort zone. That way, you won't feel pressure to make decisions on the fly, and you will have time to mentally prep for meeting lots of new people.

Here are some of the things you can plan ahead to do with colleagues:

- Carpool to the event if it's within driving distance.

- Arrange to meet for coffee at the hotel lounge between sessions.

- Take a group walk to the closest bookstore.

- Plan an impromptu photo shoot you can all use for your websites or social media.

- Arrange to attend specific panels together.

- Divide and conquer: attend separate panels and then regroup to share notes on what you each learned.

- Find another writer and do a live social media broadcast from the event about how the conference is going and what you liked so far, to share with writers who couldn't make it that year.

My own experience of attending conferences led me to create with Brittany Dowdle *The Conference Notebook*. It's a notebook that I specifically use at conferences, where I keep ALL my conference notes. In this notebook I do my conference prep work like write down my goals for the event, the people I want to meet, the sessions I want to attend, my session notes and takeaways, and the follow-up work I have to do afterward. It's been a great tool to organize my conference-going experience, but also, a notebook I can go back to and specifically revisit my notes about specific presenters or sessions. (You can find this handy notebook at thenetworkingstudio.com/books.)

Be Prepared

If you don't have *The Conference Notebook*, another good way to prep for in-person conference networking is to have business cards made well ahead of time and to write out conference note-cards for yourself. What are conference notecards? Imagine having a small stack of 3 x 5 cards that you can flip through on the plane (or a list in the Notes section of your phone). On one card is your elevator pitch, on another is a list of three of your favorite projects, on another is a list of three of your most well-known projects. One card might have a getting-to-know-you series of questions to ask new connections, and another might have a list of current news topics in the industry. Nerdy, you say? Maybe so, but it's better to embrace your inner nerd than to draw a blank when the fifth person asks what your specialty is, or someone asks whether you've written anything they know.

Being prepared to network is a key part of my approach to networking. It allows you to make well-thought-out, mindful decisions that align with your goals before you ever venture out into the world. And it puts you in a position of confidence and ease so that you don't feel rushed, on the spot, or intimidated. That way, you'll be more comfortable being you—and that's what effective networking is about.

A WRITER'S PERSPECTIVE

I teach and speak at a lot of writing conferences, retreats, workshops, and events. The one thing I have consistently found is that the writing community is an incredible group filled with intelligent, dynamic, and intriguing people. Within a few minutes of meeting another writer we can passionately explore for hours the innerworkings of our latest creations. We can brainstorm something we are struggling with and another writer will offer a brilliant solution to something that has eluded us for six months. We discuss the process, the flow, the anxieties and struggles, and the joys and bright spots. We go deep. We give suggestions to elevate another's prose and we receive clarity on things we couldn't see on our own. We reach within and give our time, energy, and talent to help strangers to keep them moving forward with their journey. Those strangers do the same for us. The beauty of this community is that writers are about collaboration, not competition. Connecting with other writers is one of my favorite aspects of what I do because writing is not a solo endeavor, it is a shared activity. We need each other.

—**CHERIE KEPHART,** EDITOR, WRITING FACILITATOR,

AND AWARD-WINNING AUTHOR OF *A Few Minor Adjustments*

Writer Check-In:

Adie was a member of a few writing organizations when she first started out, but the dues were high and she felt lost in a big sea of veteran writers. Her professional-organization comparison tool showed that there are other affordable groups that are smaller and have a reputation for high-quality continuing education. And there are free options that are known for being supportive and welcoming of writers who specialize in genre fiction by indie authors. She's going to choose three groups to try out, and she'll reassess the situation in a year.

Adie's Action Items for Professional Organizations:

1. Join the Science Fiction and Fantasy Writers Association (SFWA); visit their site and read about what's new on a weekly basis.

2. Sign up for five webinars on topics that will help me grow as a writer.

3. Join a local writers' meetup (or my local NaNoWriMo chapter) and connect intentionally with other writers.

Quarterly Networking Worksheet

Action Items for My Professional Organizations:

_____

_____

_____

_____

_____

_____

_____

A WRITER'S PERSPECTIVE

My picture book series, *Momma Comma and Friends*, would not be what it is without the support and input of the teachers, parents, and children who have read them. People often think that networking is about getting yourself and your work in front of industry professionals or colleagues, and while that may be necessary and helpful, as an independent author and illustrator, I like to use most of my energy to connect with my readers. Their enthusiasm has opened doors to local elementary schools, where I've been invited to read and sell my books. I've always greatly enjoyed my interactions with the kids and have been grateful for opportunities to meet their teachers. While I have a website and a Facebook and Instagram account, in-person events have always been so satisfying, productive, and meaningful. This is how I think about networking, which makes it less about promoting myself and more about the community.

—**LEEJONE WONG,** AUTHOR OF *Momma Comma and Friends*

CHAPTER 9

NETWORKING TACTIC #5
VOLUNTEERING

> *It takes a village to produce a book. Without alpha readers, critique group members, editorial professionals, beta readers, ARC reviewers, and fans, it's hard to build a solid career as an indie author. But, through digital and in-person networking, and volunteering, indie authors can create communities of scribes, readers, and publishing experts who can support them as they work toward realizing their unique definition of successful authorship.*
>
> —TENESHA CURTIS, AUTHOR OF INTRO TO INDIE PUBLISHING & SCAPEG.O.A.T.

Have you ever noticed how people come alive when they're working on something they're passionate about? In the best cases, when people volunteer, insecurities drop away, the ego takes a back seat, and everyone is united by a common goal. No one *has* to be there, but everyone present *wants* to be there. Each person has something to contribute and looks forward to giving their time, energy, and talents to accomplish some good—something that will benefit others.

That's the starting place for volunteering—the desire to give your best to help a like-minded group achieve goals that will benefit the community. Most people volunteer because they believe in a community or a specific goal, and they want to contribute. And in any volunteer work you do, that initial kernel of a giving spirit is critical. It's what puts you on the path.

But as I've discovered, volunteering, particularly in professional groups, is also a networking supercharger. No matter where you are in your career—from a newbie to a veteran—you can volunteer. And in doing so, you can expand and strengthen your network.

Volunteering can

- give you an inside perspective of your professional community (i.e., the Asian American Writers' Workshop or the American Society of Journalists and Authors) or of your ideal reader's community (like the Historical Novel Society if you write historical romance or thrillers);

- give you the opportunity to meet others who are on the same career path but at different points in their journeys, which can be enlightening for both the newbie and the veteran and even lead to collaborations;

- help you build your brand and become known among prospective readers, or potential clients and those who might refer work to you;

- make you an expert—even if it's in one little corner of your professional world (a former crime reporter I know, after leaving the newspaper he worked at, now writes true crime novels);

- help you discover colleagues who could be part of your small, trusted network;

- keep you up to date on the current issues facing your professional niche—and give you the chance to become part of the solution;

- increase the likelihood of your being top of mind when someone needs to give a client a referral in your specialty;

- increase your confidence and sense of satisfaction; and

- allow you to get out of your comfort zone and learn something new.

OPPORTUNITIES ARE EVERYWHERE

If you join a professional group that feels like "your people," one where you feel welcome, encouraged, and supported, at some point you'll find an opportunity to volunteer. Your first instinct might be to jump in. *This is so important to our group*, you think. *This is a chance to help others...* But then the part of yourself that's in charge of the calendar steps in. *Wait a minute, we don't have time for this!* And so the debate begins.

While *not* overcommitting is important (more on that in the next section), you might find it helpful to frame volunteer work as a chance to both give good and get good.

In other words, volunteering can be personally satisfying *and* amplify your networking efforts at the same time. It can bring a sense of community that's often missing in the remote working environment many of us are accustomed to, allowing you to build lateral relationships and learn from others in a low-pressure atmosphere. Quite often, specialized skills aren't required for volunteering; what's most important to volunteer coordinators is to have reliable people who do solid work and don't create drama. So, volunteering is an especially valuable opportunity for early-career professionals who are still trying to find their place and might not have the confidence that comes with experience.

One caveat in all this is that even though you're not getting paid for your volunteer work, for the networking-supercharger properties to be effective, you need to do your best work (within the time constraints, etc.). Remember, your main purpose is to help the group accomplish its goals. Dot the i's and cross the t's. Be the person who gets stuff done—and done right. It's not that you have to do *all* the things (burnout is real); it's that you want to honor your commitments.

And in doing so, you'll be building your brand—making a name for yourself as that ghostwriter who's dependable and gets details right... as that academic writer who's the queen of follow-up... as that SF/horror writer who keeps the Zoom meeting from continually spiraling out of control. And when it comes time to refer clients or readers, share opportunities, or invite a presenter to the next conference, you just might be at the top of the list.

Because we don't live on an island—and no writer *is* an island—we all have interests outside of the writing world. Think outside the box and tap into the other areas of life you enjoy. What are your hobbies? Is there a local group you belong to that could use your help and expertise? Maybe there's an opportunity at the animal shelter, or a knitting group, or a motorcycle enthusiast association. Have you tried connecting with a local food pantry or women's shelter? How about a community nonprofit? Or an advocacy group? The opportunities and organizations are endless—and usually within reach.

A WRITER'S PERSPECTIVE

In my own experience, volunteering has essentially built the foundation of my network. I've been a member of the Editorial Freelancers Association (EFA) since 2011, and I've staffed the EFA table at various conferences. Because I'm also a writer—and have been working on a cozy fantasy—in 2023, I decided to attend 20 Books Vegas (now Author Nation) as I was determined to self-publish it in 2024.

When I signed up for the conference, I also signed up to volunteer at the check-in table. I was a bit anxious about being on my own, since this was the first major conference where I wouldn't be meeting up with any friends in my close network (plus I had to travel across the country!).

While volunteering at check-in that first morning, I met some fellow writers who were also volunteering. As the conference went on, we talked after sessions, met up for tea, shared what we had learned, and went to lunch together one day. I also ran into publishing colleagues I didn't know were attending, who invited me to join them for dinner. I even attended a genre dinner, even though I didn't know anyone there and it was a bit out of my comfort zone. But I decided to just go and see what it would be like. It was a bit of an experiment, but also a positive experience. The conversation was lively, and it was good to learn about what everyone was working on and looking forward to next.

I came back from the conference with a wealth of wonderful "intangible" results:

- Timely information about the self-publishing industry, and what the (financially) successful writers are doing right now.

- Volunteering at the check-in table introduced me to new, meaningful connections to writers who were at the same stage of my writing journey, and with whom I'm still in touch with today. These are writers I can offer support to, as well as my editing knowledge, and who in return are supporting me in my own writing journey, and now we can go to conferences together too.

- Valuable information about myself! It *is* possible to find a balance between being semi-introverted while also stretching my comfort zone and trying new things. It can be fun and rewarding and it helps build my confidence.

For me, volunteering continues to be a networking superconductor.

—**BRITTANY DOWDLE**, AUTHOR OF *Networking for Freelance Editors*
AND *Treasure in a Teapot (working title)*

Self-Assessment Worksheet: Volunteering

Previous volunteer experience

Pros: _____

Cons: _____

Your main goal and substeps goals

1. _____

2. _____

3. _____

Issues that matter to you personally

1. _____

2. _____

3. _____

Your top skills

1. _____

2. _____

3. _____

Possible groups and activities to volunteer with

1. _____

2. _____

3. _____

4. _____

5. _____

6. _____

7. _____

8. _____

9. _____

10. _____

List three to five opportunities that further at least one business goal, one issue you care about, and one of your top skills. (Choose one and commit to it for six months to one year, then reassess.)

1. _____

2. _____

3. _____

4. _____

5. _____

EVALUATING YOUR VOLUNTEER WORK

In an ideal world, we could spend all our time working for the causes we believe in, and our best efforts would always pay off. But the reality is that most of us have to balance paid work with volunteer endeavors, and even when we do our best, the results don't always match our hopes, which can lead to burnout.

I've been there, as have many of the people I've volunteered with. When you believe in a cause, it's hard to say no. Especially if that "no" might mean that an important program is put on hold or that planned resources take longer to produce. At some point, you may feel like if you don't do it, it won't get done. While these are challenges that all volunteer groups have to contend with, it's important to start with yourself and identify what's within your power.

So, here are a few things you can do to evaluate your volunteer activities and avoid volunteer burnout:

- Learn as much as you can about the volunteer opportunity you're considering. How many hours does it require and how long of a commitment is it? Do you have to be on-site? Is there a clearly defined job description?

- Decide up front how much time you can commit to volunteer work (on a daily, weekly, monthly, quarterly basis) and stick to it. Don't overcommit!

- Be strategic and targeted. If you're volunteering for your local rabbit rescue, you don't have to be as strategic about it. Bunnies are bunnies. But if you're volunteering with professional or client-facing organizations, and it's part of your professional networking, then be strategic about which groups you volunteer with and which kinds of projects you take on. For instance, I help facilitate breakout rooms during IBPA member meetings, so I don't commit all my volunteer hours to my son's middle school classroom events. 1) That's not where my passion is (please don't despise me!), and 2) that's not where my people are (I care about the kids, I just don't have the vocational patience).

- Don't take on emotional responsibility beyond your role. As a volunteer, you commit to specific tasks and time commitments. Be clear about what you can do, and let the group adjust its goals based on its volunteer resources.

INSIGHT: NETWORKING INCLUSIVELY

Because the best networking is built on relationships, community, and being free to be your true self, it's critical to find and create networking spaces that are safe for all community members.

As we've learned throughout this workbook, we each have our own networking style—the place where our comfort level, natural communication style, and external engagement efforts align. For some of us, that's on social media platforms like TikTok and Facebook—for others, it's in one-on-one meetups or at conferences. While it's good to challenge yourself, it's also valuable to know what works for you and network in places (virtual and in person) where you feel comfortable.

Sometimes, though, it takes work to create those places—both for yourself and for others. And an environment that feels safe and welcoming to one person may be inimical to another person. Sometimes this comes down to personality (of the group and the individual), and sometimes it comes down to culture and identity—and how accepting people are of each other. Is the group welcoming and inclusive or off-putting and implicitly exclusionary?

Obviously, it's a complicated issue—and not one that can be fully addressed within the scope of this book—but it's important enough that we need to acknowledge that networking is influenced by cultural factors (see recommended reading resources in appendix B for more about this). A space that feels safe for one of us might be inhospitable for another. Regardless of where you fall in the interconnected web of human identity, it's important to take care *of yourself* and take care *for others*. This awareness is a necessary part of building a vibrant network.

To that end, here are a few thoughts:

- Before joining a group, talk to its members. Find out whether it's welcoming and inclusive, whether it has issues with member retention, or whether there are subgroups within the main organization that are explicitly supportive (like a new-member Diversity, Equity, and Inclusion [DEI] group).

- Look at the group's website or "About" page and read the subtext. What's important to you? Is it important to them?

- Search out groups that are a good fit for you, and consider building/joining a micro community within a group that has potential but isn't there yet.

- Ask your trusted network which groups and platforms they belong to. What have their experiences been?

- Develop direct relationships with people who are also in a group you want to join; that way, even if you're a newbie, you're a newbie with friends and a built-in support network.

- If you're able to, speak up when you witness bullying or aggressive language. This might mean alerting a moderator, reaching out to the person being attacked, or calling out the bullying directly. Be safe and do what's within your ability.

- Listen to your own instincts. Your perceptions are valid.

- Keep searching. Be willing to create the place you seek, even if it's on a small scale, like a private mastermind group.

- If you're not sure how to support others, ask them. Then listen.

LINDA RUGGERI'S PERSPECTIVE

My level of involvement in nonprofit volunteer work has changed over the years. I started off signing up for many different committees and initiatives because I knew those organizations needed help getting projects off the ground. But in turn, I spread myself too thin, and not everything I was involved with had my heart in it or aligned with my values. Over time I realized that some of the volunteer work I'd committed to doing felt more like unpaid work and wasted time.

Instead of complaining, dropping out, or ghosting them, I always try to find a solution because it's the professional thing to do. If the solution I can offer doesn't work, and the volunteer work is cutting into my paid work too much or causing levels of unmanageable stress (therefore affecting my health), then I graciously give at least a two-month notice and try to find someone else to take my place. Like any paid job, you want to leave with the best possible relationship because you never know when your paths will cross again, and who is going to need who.

For example, a committee I volunteered for had unnecessarily long monthly meetings. I dreaded being on the calls because time is at a premium for me as a full-time freelancer and a mom. But I also felt bad if I didn't participate in the meetings. So, I stepped up and offered to facilitate some of the meetings. You'd think I would have added more to my plate, but not really. I studied the book *The 25 Minute Meeting,* implemented an online, itemized, timed agenda, and asked that everyone write their short report in the agenda *before* the meeting. That way, we could bypass giving reports unless anyone had a question about them. That allowed us to streamline the conversation to things that actually had to be discussed and where decisions needed to be made. Initially, my agenda was met with a lot of resistance by the committee heads, but in the long run it was appreciated by all participants because we were able to get more done in less time, and we were being mindful of everyone's time as well.

The people I've met while volunteering at these organizations continue to refer writing and editing work to me, and I to them. We continue to stay in touch and our paths cross all the time at conferences and events. Again, volunteering is a networking superpower that will pay off for years to come.

Writer Check-In:

Realizing she never thought of volunteering as a networking superpower, Adie, who wants to connect with more mystery writers and readers, has decided to get out of her comfort zone (and away from a screen) and meet new potential readers. She'll create a plan where she can help others by sharing what she knows about the genre while also stretching a little bit out of her current comfort zone. She knows she's not volunteering to find new best friends, but because talking with others about the books she's reading comes naturally and brings her joy. And maybe that conversation exchange of shared interests is exactly what someone else needs to feel seen or heard. Adie also understands that volunteering doesn't have to be all-consuming, and she can rearrange her plan if she's not getting the results she's looking for. But, at the end of three months, she will have expanded her connections and gained a new experience stretching her comfort zone.

Adie's Action Items for Volunteering:

1. Visit the libraries in my area (or university or college libraries) and ask if they have a mystery book club I can join. If they don't, I'll ask if I can start one and how. I'll also ask what mystery books get checked out the most, and why they think that is (target audience research from a library's perspective).

2. Find and join a local writers' organization or publisher (not necessarily mystery-related) that has tables at book fairs and volunteer to staff the booth for a few hours at their next event.

3. Find an organization that does something I'm passionate about and offer to help facilitate their online meetings, annual conference, or fundraising events, or help with one of their social media platforms.

Quarterly Networking Worksheet

Action Items for My Volunteer Activities:

_____

_____

_____

_____

_____

_____

_____

_____

_____

CHAPTER 10
PERSONAL NETWORKING STYLE

If we create networks with the sole intention of getting something, we won't succeed. We can't pursue the benefits of networks, the benefits ensue from investments in meaningful activities and relationships.

—ADAM GRANT, AUTHOR OF HIDDEN POTENTIAL

In part 1 we looked at setting goals and identifying potential network members in order to reach those goals. Then in part 2 we reviewed the five networking tactics that you can use to build relationships with the people you need to connect with. For each tactic, you brainstormed steps to take and added them to your Quarterly Networking Worksheet. Based on what you've discovered, it might make sense to say: my goals *plus* the people I need to reach *equals* the networking tactics I need to use.

MY GOALS
+ THE PEOPLE I NEED TO REACH

THE NETWORKING TACTICS I NEED TO USE

However, that formula is missing a critical element. While it's important to have specific networking goals and plans in place, you also need to consider your natural communication preferences so that you'll *do the plan* and *reach your goals*. This is especially true for introverts. As networking expert Devora Zack explains, "Everybody is more than fine as they are. When we tap rather than cap our true nature, the sky is the limit." What does this mean? It means we don't have to change who we are; we are enough just the way we are. The secret, then, is recognizing and acknowledging to ourselves what type of networking we are comfortable with, and what type of networking we would not enjoy.

So the real formula is: my goals *plus* the people I need to reach *plus* my networking style *equals* the networking tactics I need to use.

MY GOALS
+ THE PEOPLE I NEED TO REACH
+ MY NETWORKING STYLE

THE NETWORKING TACTICS I NEED TO USE

Before working on the following self-assessment, look at your current network snapshot in chapter 2 to see where you've been networking up to this point. What you find there might indicate your baseline networking comfort zone.

A WRITER'S PERSPECTIVE

More and more, academics seem to be engaging in promotion of their work on platforms like social media. Sometimes there will be official accounts for research groups where they'll promote the group's work or talk about other relevant work in the field, and these can generally be seen as a networking tool for the group as a whole. Individual researchers also do this, for example, Duncan Sproul (@sproul_lab). I do not believe there is any requirement or formal expectation on principal investigators or other researchers to do this, but getting your name out there helps make the research group/principal investigator attractive to potential PhD students and postdocs; helps attract collaborators; and can affect other opportunities, too, such as book deals or career advancement possibilities.

The same goes for attending conferences and giving presentations. Whether a presentation of research at a conference takes place before or after that research is published in a journal (or these occur simultaneously) will depend on the field; but those presentations give attendees the opportunity to ask questions that can generate important discussion or facilitate future collaborations, and they also generate exposure to new potential readers.

For some journals the readership is going to be there, no matter what. But getting published in those is difficult, and the audience is not very specialised because the journals are pretty broad in scope. So networking continues to be important. Some academic fields are very narrow, and may not have many members; if those fields only have a few publication venues, it may be easy to find the audience. But if you're an academic in a very specialised subfield of, say, geology, that doesn't have its own journal(s), your network and self-promotion activities might be crucial to getting your work in front of your peers.

—**BAILEY HARRINGTON,** PHD, WRITER, EDITOR,

AND OWNER OF GREENPEN EDITING

Self-Assessment Worksheet: Personal Networking Style

What are your *preferred* ways to network? _____

_____

Where do you feel most comfortable?

      In-person socializing (conferences, chapter meetings, literary festivals)?

      Video and phone (webinars, virtual groups, mastermind groups)?

      Email?

      Online discussion lists and forums?

      Social media: LinkedIn, Facebook, Twitter, Pinterest?

What new way of networking would you like to try? _____

_____

What type of networking is of no interest to you? (This doesn't mean no forever, just no for now.)

_____

If you dread the idea of networking, what specific activities are you thinking of?

_____

_____

_____

_____

Describe a networking plan that focuses on your preferred networking activities and is light on the ones you don't like doing.

_____

_____

_____

_____

_____

A WRITER'S PERSPECTIVE

I know that many people view networking as a chore and a burden. Me too. I used to think, oh no, I have to put myself out there and face potential rejection and what do I even say? Over time and with a lot of practice, I've come to see networking from a different perspective, one that focuses on the joy that comes from new, vibrant, productive connections. So many times, I've met writers here or there and subsequently published their stories in the *Made in L.A.* anthologies. Or I've been introduced to someone by a colleague and then a speaking opportunity or an editing gig comes my way. In publishing, we live in a kind of ecosystem that's not eat or be eaten. Instead, it's about contributing together in the creation of something beautiful. Like, you bring the water, I'll bring the sun, and we'll grow this tree together and enjoy its fruits: enjoyable books, interesting conversations, and lifelong relationships.

—**CODY SISCO,** AUTHOR, EDITOR,

AND PUBLISHER OF *Made in L.A.* ANTHOLOGY SERIES

EXPLORING YOUR STYLE

Acknowledging and leveraging your personal networking style is the secret ingredient to making a networking plan that will work for you. Networking—putting yourself out there, meeting new people—it's all challenging enough without having to fight against your natural tendencies. So, work with what you have—and who you are right now. Maybe you just don't get TikTok, and if you have to become a TikTok pro, your networking plan is doomed before it even starts. But LinkedIn is your zone—you've gained three clients through LinkedIn and helped four colleagues connect with awesome opportunities. In that case, use your expertise and get creative. Make the most of your strengths. And maybe in a year you'll decide that you're ready to learn to post with the best of them. Who knows? That great connection you made on LinkedIn may need help getting their LinkedIn game up to speed, but they're a natural on TikTok. Help each other out! Teach each other how to make these platforms work for your needs.

Or maybe you don't like getting dressed up and going to conferences. Perhaps you find travel exhausting or you need to stay home to help care for a family member. Today, none of that has to limit your ability to make connections and build your network. You can sign up for virtual conferences, attend video meetings, or reach colleagues on the other side of the world—all without leaving your home.

There's no one right way to network. Do what you're comfortable with today, and respect what makes you "you." When you start in your comfort zone and make the most of it, you'll develop the confidence to exceed it—if you wish to (or, you may find you're exactly where you need to be).

FINDING BALANCE

Now is the time to take your completed Quarterly Networking Worksheet and place it beside the Personal Networking Style self-assessment. Your answers to this chapter's self-assessment worksheet will help you establish which networking tactics to pursue.

Do the networking tactics you've sketched out in the quarterly plan align with your personal comfort and productivity zones? Highlight the networking actions that might be a challenge for you based on your personal style. (You might think of these as residing in your "growth zone," a place of challenge and possibility.) Notice that I'm not suggesting you cross the growth-zone actions off your list. I'm just asking you to highlight them so you're aware of where your internal resistance might rear its head. If you've done the exercises throughout the workbook and put in the time and thought to craft a good plan, then believe in the plan.

Writer Check-In:

As Adie worked through the answers to the Personal Networking Style self-assessment, she realized that she enjoys interacting on Facebook and Instagram, but she has difficulty finding a balanced tone in emails. Adie also recognized that virtual spaces are much more comfortable for her than the prospect of attending meetings or conferences in person. She's had the opportunity to attend many events virtually, but she feels that to move her career forward, she needs to be more comfortable with in-person gatherings.

As she reviews her completed Quarterly Networking Worksheet, she uses this knowledge of her networking style to guide her efforts and shape her networking strategy for the next quarter. Because she knows that she'll be testing this plan for the next three months, after which she'll assess her progress, Adie has the freedom to experiment and be intentional about networking with purpose.

When we look at Adie's plan on the next pages, we see she has managed to include three of the five networking tactics: website (blog post), social media (Facebook and Instagram), and professional groups (PEN America and Sisters in Crime). She's also going to attend a low-stress in-person event at her local library to acclimate herself to in-person networking. During each of these networking activities, Adie will keep in mind how they will help her achieve her goals of working with indie mystery authors, establishing her reputation as a writer, and building her unique brand. The actual planned networking she does each week will shift according to her available time and the opportunities she finds to contribute to her network's growth and success, but her daily mindset—being giving, adding value, and connecting with others—remains active and constant.

Below is what Adie's spreadsheet might look like for week 1 of her first quarter. Note, it might not seem like a lot at first, but if you're someone who has a full-time job doing something else, or if you're only writing part-time, this will be a lot to accomplish in one week. But Adie is serious about trying a new system and really committing to it for a month. If by week 2 or week 3 the activities feel shallow or unsustainable, she will tailor them down to something that works better for her, or alternate these activities between weeks.

WEEK 1	Activity	Time Allocated	Who Am I Reaching?
Monday	Join PEN America. Craft a directory profile that reflects my focus on mystery and related genres.	2 hours	Fellow writers who are working in the industry.
Tuesday	Start a short blog post (800 words) titled "How to Create a Red Herring in Your Mystery." Talk about this on Instagram and Facebook; ask followers for their favorite literary red herring.	1 hour	Mystery writers, past clients, potential clients, and readers of mystery fiction.

Wednesday	Search for indie authors who specialize in mystery. Choose five. Follow them on social media, look over their books, and check out their websites. Comment on one mystery-related post for each of them.	1 hour	Indie authors, other authors, novice writers who are fans of these indie brands.
Thursday	Join Sisters in Crime, explore the member area, and search for the closest local chapter (or an online chapter).	30 minutes	Mystery authors and authors.
Friday	Finish blog post, have colleague proofread it. Post on website. Share on social media (Facebook and Instagram). Attend a mystery author chat at a local library or bookstore.	1.5 to 3 hours	Mystery writers and authors, readers, aspiring writers.

Quarterly Networking Worksheet

Action Items for My Personal Networking Style:

_____

_____

_____

_____

_____

_____

CHAPTER 11

AVOIDING NETWORKING PITFALLS

Altruism, good manners, and kindness always pay off.

— BRITTANY DOWDLE AND LINDA RUGGERI, *THE NETWORKING STUDIO COMMUNITY*

Over the years, as an active member in the writing and editing communities in the US and abroad, I've tried to put my best efforts forward when meeting with clients, colleagues, and professionals who work in the publishing industry. I've attended conferences, volunteered for local chapters, hosted networking meetings, taken classes, participated in webinars and panels, and written blog posts. I've hired colleagues, referred colleagues, and been the recipient of referrals. In each situation, I've tried to engage mindfully with everyone who crossed my path.

But I know there are times I've missed the mark, when my best efforts at the time weren't good enough. With all the positives that have come from my career as a writer, editor, and translator, I've also observed a lot of behaviors that were less than appealing, and inadvertently, I've surely been guilty of some of the same and have had to make amends because the relationship was important to me.

While it's easy to pick up on these behaviors in someone else, it can be tough to recognize them in ourselves. Networking turnoffs I've experienced include bad attitudes, negativity, a lack of commitment, subpar work, blatant selfishness, the absence of empathy, and a focus on "networking-as-transaction." I've been on calls where my name, or the name of my book, was butchered, or where the interviewer wasn't really interested in what I had to say and was doing something else as they asked me questions. These are the types of behaviors that will sabotage all our good networking efforts.

Don't burn a bridge and then expect me to send a boat.

—*AUTHOR UNKNOWN*

So, as only a true friend would celebrate our success, lift us up when we're down, and gently point out areas or conduct we might consider revising because it can hurt us, let me share seven keys to avoiding pitfalls when networking.

BE PROFESSIONAL

Professional should be your default setting (which you can later relax as you get to know people). Being professional signifies different things to different people—whether in different countries or across cultures within the same country. To some, being professional is just a matter of knowing their stuff (a specialized knowledge). For others, it's not only about the knowledge acquired through schooling and experience, but a combination of education and everyday behavior. You can't control how another person will interpret your behavior, but you can be diligent about the business persona you project and about how you react in tough situations.

I've met writers who are very knowledgeable, and financially successful, but who lack professionalism when it comes to working with clients or colleagues. What do we mean by that? Well, sometimes writers can be rude or curt. Other times they don't deliver on what they promised or are too embarrassed to admit they made a mistake and don't own up to it. Some writers will share too much personal information with people they barely know, making a colleague or client feel uncomfortable. And sometimes a lack of professionalism has nothing to do with our skills and knowledge, but someone catches us at the wrong time, when our mind is engaged somewhere else and we can't answer that question, so we give a short answer, and all of a sudden we're labeled the "bad-mannered one."

Part of being professional is balancing politeness and friendliness with boundaries. Try to be polite to everyone. However, if life happens, or there's a blowup in a forum, and you feel you can't be polite, then it's okay to simply and firmly remove yourself from the situation. We've all been there at one point in our careers. Don't let one person bring you to their level, where you'd compromise your professionalism, especially in front of others.

To maintain a professional persona, be courteous, be kind, be compassionate—and stay true to your core values. Many times, while I may be blowing up inside and wanting to yell *What is wrong with you?* at that person, I remember the Oprah Winfrey and Dr. Bruce Perry book, and try to wonder to myself instead, *What Happened to You?* That helps me put things in perspective.

BUILD YOUR SKILLS

Professionalism is also about being competent and knowing your stuff. You're competent when you can get the job done—because you know how to do the job. When you start off as a writer, you aren't all-knowing; you're still building up your skills. In fact, professionals are always building their skills—that includes veteran authors.

No one knows everything, but we can learn what we need to know to do our work at a high level. So if you're thinking about taking on a project that's not in your area of expertise or is in an area or genre you want to transition into, build your skills first: take classes, read extensively about the topic, read works in that genre or specialty, interview people who are experts in that field, and dispel every single one of your doubts. Fill up the knowledge gap. Continuous improvement should be part of your everyday work. If you're not sure where to start, check out the webinars and classes on offer through different writing, editing, and publishing organizations. A great first step is to learn about conscious language, for which you'll want to get a copy of *The Conscious Style Guide* by Karen Yin (and subscribe to the newsletter), or the *Conscious Language Toolkit for Writers* by Crystal Shelley.

RECIPROCATE WHEN POSSIBLE, SHOW GRATITUDE ALWAYS

Reciprocating kindness is a way to show your colleagues that you respect them and care about your networking relationships. If someone has passed on a potential client or vendor lead to you, make sure to show your gratitude to that colleague. If a client has hired you, at the end of that project, make sure to express how grateful you are that they chose *you* to do that work.

There are many creative ways to show gratitude; here are some of my favorites:

- Send a thank-you card. This still works! (Tip: buy your stamps at the supermarket while grocery shopping to avoid going to the post office, or get some neat Forever Stamps that align with your brand or writing area of expertise. The post office has so many wonderful choices!)

- Like someone's content on social media and share it, giving that person credit—it's free! (Share about a class or talk they are going to give, an article they've written, or a resource they've created. Share a photo of your client's book and mention where it can be bought. I like to share all types of writing and editing classes by others I follow on my Instagram and FB Stories, so it almost looks like a reel.)

- Send a gift as a thank-you for a referral. In the writing world, tea, coffee, and gift certificates to bookstores are always appreciated! Be careful not to make the gift too personal. A $35 gift for a project that earned you $350 should be considered an investment in your networking relationship. The person who referred the work to you will be grateful, and will most likely refer other work if they feel appreciated.

- Leave a review wherever you purchased the book, recommend it to someone via a LinkedIn profile post, or write a testimonial on their website. Again, this is another activity that takes a few minutes and doesn't cost anything, and the impact this can have for an author on the bookselling algorithm is enormous. As authors we need reviews to sell our books.

- Refer connections to someone else, make an introduction, or if a good opportunity comes your way, return the favor. (Again, free!)

IMAGE MATTERS

The saying "You only have one chance to make a first impression" couldn't be truer. Make that first impression work for you! That means curating your words, your image, your attitude, your workspace. If a client or colleague senses that you don't take care of yourself and your business, they'll assume you're not going to take care of them or their project.

Be professional in your appearance. That doesn't mean having fancy attire, but it does mean minding personal hygiene, wearing clean clothes, and respecting the fact that many clients work in traditional offices and hold certain expectations. (Note: This general advice speaks to the realities of interacting with clients and colleagues and to general ideas of what is considered "professional," but I also want to recognize that "professional" is a cultural construct that can sometimes make us feel like we have to hide who we are or change who we are to be accepted. So my advice is: Be true to yourself and put your best effort forward. The colleagues you want to associate with will appreciate who you are. The clients who will enrich your professional life will value the real you.)

When you're working, be professional in every possible way. Keep your speech mindful and respectful, even if you don't agree with people's work styles or opinions. I try to avoid discussing religion, politics, or other sensitive subjects unless they are related to the project I am working on. Many times we might not know our client or colleague's background and what they may find offensive, so it's best to avoid sticky situations.

If you know you're going to be on a video call, choose your space carefully! Many of us are multitasking at home with other family members. Our spaces can be busy, but let's make sure they're tidy. Orderly spaces tell our clients a lot about us and the way we work. And they do notice. And an untidy space is not only distracting, but unprofessional when you're on a business call.

If you need to take a video call or host a meeting from your phone, find a good space and prop up your phone ahead of time. If your surroundings are unconventional, that's okay. Just keep in mind that colleagues and clients expect us to be attentive, to be active listeners, and to engage with them.

RESPECT OTHER PEOPLE'S TIME, SPACE, AND PREFERENCES

If you're communicating with someone new, it's a good idea to use email first. Once you begin to understand the relationship, and if you prefer, ask whether they'd like to also communicate by text, video, or phone. Don't assume, and never text someone without asking for permission to do so first.

Avoid sending urgent requests at night or on the weekends. Be mindful that people have lives outside of work and may not appreciate hearing from you during that time. If you do need help from someone during those times, then make sure your request is specific—make it easy for people to help you.

Remember, your clients and colleagues may live in different time zones than you, and your phone call or text message may come in when they're sleeping or having dinner with their family. You don't want to be the person who is texting or calling at that time. (For example, I live on the West Coast and at times I get text messages in the wee hours of the morning from clients on the East Coast who completely disregard the time zone.)

PERSONAL INFORMATION

As mentioned earlier, wait to share personal information until you develop a relationship that supports that level of sharing. If you're too informal and reveal one of your shortcomings or insecurities to a client, they may be reticent to hire you for future projects. There is a space and time for everything.

However, keep in mind that other cultures feel differently about this, and they may ask you personal questions first to establish a working relationship before they move on to discuss business topics. As a Latina with a South American upbringing, we are more interested in getting to know you first (what you do for fun, if you have a family or kids, what you did over the weekend) before we are ready to discuss work. You don't have to reveal everything about yourself, but you can keep your answer slightly personal and short because for us it's a way to build trust with the people we're working with.

Finally, as a freelancer, you know how much time and effort you've put into building your business, making contacts, developing your processes, and winning clients. While more experienced professionals are often happy to give back and share their hard-won knowledge with colleagues who are just starting out, recognize this generosity as the gift it is. And respect their boundaries; in other words, don't respond to someone's kindness by blatantly asking for their client contact list or demanding to know what they charge (and yes, it happens all the time). If you've benefited from someone's help, remember to pass the favor on. Generosity is the fabric networks are made of.

LEARN TO FAIL FORWARD

Sometimes, even with our best intentions and planning, things can go wrong. We unintentionally hurt someone through our words or actions; we make a mistake. When that happens, our practice should be to stop and take a moment to reflect. I usually consult with one or two trusted colleagues. I choose my next steps wisely. And if I need to apologize, I do—because it's important to own up to our failures just as much as to our successes.

No one in our industry has all the knowledge. We're all learning and evolving. When we're able to understand why we're in the wrong, and then make amends, people respect us, and we're better for doing so. We all move forward together. As Crystal Shelley states in her *Conscious Language Toolkit*, "While intent is important in helping us decide how to craft our message, it doesn't change how our message is received." Being mindful of the other person and seeking to lift others up is a core aspect of effective networking and sharing spaces—whether real or virtual—with others.

CHAPTER 12

FOR AUTHORS SELLING BOOKS

In the introduction of this book, I mentioned this was not a workbook intended exclusively to teach book authors how to network, and that it is also not a book about how to sell more books. However, it would be foolish of me not to acknowledge that networking as an author is just as important as writing the book itself, because it takes a good, solid team of people to make a book happen.

Books don't magically float into a reader's hands, and a reader's money doesn't magically flow into the author's bank account. Those two simple actions take time and a boatload of people with knowledge to make them happen. For a book to be published, in any shape, form, format, or platform, and *then* for it to reach its intended readers (let alone make a profit) you will need experienced, intelligent, reliable, and sentient human beings in your network to help you make that happen.[5]

As a writer of books myself, and having experienced firsthand, to some successful degree, the indie-publishing market, I can only share what I know, and what I wish someone would have told me when I considered writing my first book. Please don't consider this a game plan but just a brief introduction to the subject. You may not need to have all these people in your network, but you'd be wise to start building those connections and keeping them close if you intend on publishing more than one book. One other thing to note is that some of them will fit better into your close network (i.e., a trusted editor you can consult with during writing and during revisions) and some of them may fit better into your broad network (i.e., a local offset printer who can print rack cards on short notice for the author tables you choose to be at).

---

5   Sure, AI can help you automate and enhance many things for your book, but AI is not your target audience, so if you decide to use it, tread carefully and know its limitations and the legalities involved with its use. Remember that your expectations of what AI can give your writing or publishing process may not be your readers' expectations of *your* writing.

People You Should Connect With

Editors (developmental editors, line editors, and copyeditors that edit in your genre and are familiar with conscious language so you're not alienating any readers)

Proofreaders

Book cover designers (who understand not only the book market you're publishing in but also the psychology of your target readers' book purchasing behavior)

Interior book designers (who understand accessibility)

Epub book coders (who also understand accessibility and how screen readers work for your readers who are visually impaired)

Audiobook producers

Author website designers

Distribution partners (i.e., contacts at IngramSpark, Draft2Digital, BookBaby, Lulu, Baker & Taylor, and Kindle Direct Publishing—good luck with that last one!)

Local librarians

Book clubs

Writing conference organizers

Book festival/fair organizers

Alpha and beta readers (before your manuscript is finalized)

ARC (advance reader copy) readers, a street team, or book reviewing sites (i.e., NetGalley) after your manuscript has been properly edited

Book award organizations

Translators or foreign rights agents

Book marketing consultant

Social media consultant

An accountant and lawyer who understand the publishing world

As I continue to grow as a writer, author, and author-publisher, I keep discovering other professionals I want to connect with, collaborate with, and have in my network, and you will to.

People You Should Connect With

Get Your Book Selling at Events and Signings by Monica Leonelle and Russell P. Nohelty

Networking for Authors: How to Make Friends, Sell More Books and Grow a Publishing Network from Scratch by Dan Parsons

The Author Stylist Guide by Jennifer Milius, writer, editor, and author stylist

Get Your Book Selling on Kickstarter by Monica Leonelle and Russell P. Nohelty

The Business of Being a Writer by Jane Friedman

The Bestselling Book Formula and *You Must Write a Book* by Honorée Corder

Perfect Bound: How to Navigate the Book Publishing Process Like a Pro and *Publishing Resources for Authors, Editors, and Publishers* by Katherine Pickett

Intro to Indie Publishing by Tenesha Curtis

Joanna Penn (her whole collection is fantastic)

BookBub's "The Ultimate Collection of Book Marketing Examples"

Lastly, I also want to reassure you that it only takes setting up these connections once, because you will most likely continue to work with them over and over again. And as you grow as a published author, you'll continue to add new experts to your network.

A WRITER'S PERSPECTIVE

There's nothing like face-to-face networking. Particularly in Washington. Stop by any coffee store in DC and you'll overhear job interviews, staff meetings, first dates, lobbyist presentations, even writer meetups. The whole town seems to be networking! Since my fiction takes place in Washington, it's super important for me to keep my contacts fresh. I attend the Congressional Baseball Game to run into members of Congress who agreed to write blurbs for my books. Last year, one of my congressional contacts didn't have time for coffee, but he got me a front row seat at the January 6th hearings! I make coffee dates with researchers at the White House Historical Society and U.S. Capitol Historical Society (USCHS) and a blogger at the Library of Congress who have terrific ideas for stories and best practice suggestions for research. I stop by all the Capitol Hill gift shops to pitch my books in person. (Even when they say no, the shop buyer will say, "Oh, yes. You're the girl who writes those Fina Mendoza books.") Face-to-face encounters are the ones people remember. It's easy for emails to get buried in an inbox. If at all possible, network in person. And buy the coffee!

—**Kitty Felde,** fORMER NPR JOURNALIST AND
AUTHOR OF *Welcome to Washington, Fina Mendoza*

CONCLUSION

Thank you for buying this book and working through it with me. My hope is that through the work you've done, you have a new understanding of what networking can be—and how it can help you reach your goals.

Now you have a new perspective—one that puts you at the center of a positive, interconnected web of colleagues, clients, and future friends. In this dynamic web, your personal communication style—your comfort zone—isn't something you have to overcome, but rather, it's the foundation for your signature networking style. And the more connections you make by embracing your unique style, the stronger your network will be, because it's an organic extension of who you are—not who you think you should be in order to be a networking superstar.

You know this, but I'll say it again: networking success isn't measured by the number of people you know, the size of your digital footprint, or how many LinkedIn connections or TikTok followers you have. Instead of comparing yourself to the most visible authors on social media or the most outgoing person at the latest conference, consider the network you started with—and the network you are building for yourself. If your networking is helping you reach your professional goals, then it's a success. It's that simple.

Because we're all at different stages of our careers, the main portion of this book focused on the most important aspects of my approach to networking—assessing your needs, understanding the five core networking tactics, and discovering your personal networking style. I've reserved specific how-to tips and in-depth resources for the appendixes and for the book's website, where you'll find practical starter tips, best practices, courses, study groups, and other tools to help you begin your networking journey. And remember, you aren't alone. There is a community of writing professionals out there just like you, waiting to be found, heard, read, and supported.

A final reminder: networking occurs between living, sentient beings in the midst of evolving technology and resources. This book will never be an exhaustive analysis of what we can accomplish together, but it's a start. If you have suggestions, ideas, or corrections—or would like to continue the conversation with me—I'd love to hear from you at www.thenetworkingstudio.com.

Wishing you much success!

Linda Ruggeri

ACKNOWLEDGMENTS

No book is ever the product of just one person. I have an amazing network of people I'd like to thank because they believed in me and my work. Every writer quote or story I asked for was met with an immediate "yes." Every one of them is someone I admire, who has in one way or another enlightened me with their knowledge and experience, and motivated me to make this book happen:

Bailey Harrington (www.greenpenediting.com)

Cherie Kephart (www.cheriekephart.com)

Christine Van Zandt (www.christinevanzandt.com)

Cody Sisco (www.codysisco.com)

Ebonye Gussine Wilkins, Inclusive Media Solutions, LLC (egwmedia.com)

John Peragine (www.johnpwriter.com)

Jordan Rosenfeld (www.jordanrosenfeld.net)

Katherine Pickett (www.popediting.net)

Kitty Felde (www.kittyfelde.com)

Leejone Wong (www.mommacomma.com)

Louise Harnby (www.louiseharnbyproofreader.com)

Luis Arturo Pelayo, Spanish to Move (www.spanishtomove.com)

Michelle Lowery, Sevillana Publishing, LLC (www.michellelowery.com)

Nathan Makaryk (www.nathanmakaryk.com)

Samantha Nolan, Nolan Branding (www.nolanbranding.com)

Tenesha L. Curtis (www.teneshalcurtis.com)

W. Paul Coates (www.agooddaytoprint.com)

And Ran Walker (www.ranwalker.com), for his generosity of heart, of time, and of wisdom: "Consider saying yes to the things that you're afraid of when the only thing holding you back is fear."

Finally, a heartfelt thank you to my editor, Kelly Young, for her amazing insights and care with my words. To Melinda Martin for her exquisite graphic design and attention to detail, always keeping the reader's needs at the forefront. To my family who seem to support me unconditionally while never really knowing quite what I do. And to Brittany Dowdle, with whom I will always share this book's DNA.

APPENDIX A

ORGANIZATIONS

The following are organizations that might be a good fit for you and your interests as you build your professional network. By no means is this list exhaustive or complete. For instance, if you specialize in writing content for a specific industry, such as organic agriculture or green energy, you'll want to develop a network within those fields as well.

GENERAL WRITING

Academy of American Poets

Alliance of Independent Authors

American Translators Association

Association for Women in Communications

Association of Writers and Writing Programs

Atlanta Writers Club

Authors Guild

Independent Writers of Southern California

International Women's Writing Guild

NaNoWriMo

PEN America

University of Chicago Press

Writer's Digest

Writers Guild of America East

Writers Guild of America West

SPECIFIC INTEREST WRITING

American Christian Fiction Writers (ACFW)

American Medical Writers Association (AMWA)

American Society of Journalists and Authors (ASJA)

Asian American Writers' Workshop

Authors Guild

Black Writers Collective

Children's Book Council

Children's Writer's Guild

Contemporary Romance Writers (CRW)

Dramatists Guild of America

Education Writers Association

Freelancers Union

Georgia Romance Writers

Historical Novel Society

Horror Writers Association

Independent Book Publishers Association (IBPA)

Indian Authors Association

Indigenous Journalists Association (IJA)

Institute of Children's Literature

International Food Wine and Travel Writers Association (IFWTWA)

International Society of Latino Authors (ISLA)

Mystery Writers of America

National Association of Independent Writers and Editors (NAIWE)

National Association of Science Writers (NASW)

NLGJA: The Association of LGBTQ+ Journalists

Nonfiction Authors Association

Poetry Foundation

Poetry Society of America

Poets & Writers

Romance Writers of America (RWA)

Romantic Novelists' Association (RNA)

Science Fiction and Fantasy Writers Association (SFWA)

Sisters in Crime

Society for Advanced Business Editing and Writing (SABEW)

Society for Technical Communication (STC)

Society of American Travel Writers (SATW)

The Society of Authors (UK)

Society of Children's Book Writers and Illustrators (SCBWI)

Stage 32 (for screenwriters)

Trans Journalists Association

Volunteer Lawyers for the Arts (VLANY)

Western Writers of America

Women's Fiction Writers

EDITORIAL ORGANIZATIONS

ACES: The Society for Editing

American Society for Indexing

Asian Council of Science Editors

Bay Area Editors' Forum (BAEF)

Black Editors & Proofreaders

Board of Editors in the Life Sciences (BELS)

Chartered Institute of Editing and Proofreading (CIEP)

Copyediting-L (CE-L) (forum)

Council of Science Editors (CSE)

Editorial Freelancers Association (EFA)

Indigenous Editors Association

Institute of Professional Editors Limited (IPEd)

National Association of Independent Writers and Editors (NAIWE)

Professional Editors Network (PEN)

The Society of Indexers (UK)

Spanish Editors Association (SEA)

APPENDIX B

RECOMMENDED READINGS

Throughout my career, but more so when I began researching material for this book, I bought, checked out, and borrowed dozens of books related to the benefits and challenges of networking and the craft of writing. I looked for materials that would make me a wiser freelancer and creative entrepreneur, as well as solid, useful advice to help strengthen and expand my business.

The lists that follow are *not* about the craft of writing, however, you can find my preferred list of craft books on The Networking Studio's Bookshop.org page at www.bookshop.org/shop/thenetworkingstudio.

The books below have shown me not only great approaches to networking and owning a business while being a writer, but also corroborated my thoughts that *it is possible* to live a more meaningful professional and personal life by authentically connecting with others. I hope you enjoy these books just as much as I did.

NETWORKING

Build Your Dream Network by J. Kelly Hoey

Connect First by Melanie A. Katzman

Give and Take by Adam Grant

Joy at Work by Marie Kondo and Scott Sonenshein

Networking for Authors by Dan Parsons

Networking for People Who Hate Networking by Devora Zack

Networking Magic by Rick Frishman and Jill Lublin

Quiet: The Power of Introverts in a World That Can't Stop Talking by Susan Cain

The 11 Laws of Likability by Michelle Tillis Lederman

ACCESSIBILITY

"Alt Text for SEO: How to Optimize Your Images"
    (ahrefs.com/blog/alt-text)

" 'Born Accessible' Publishing"
  (pensite.org/2021/05/born-accessible-publishing)

"Everything You Need to Know to Write Effective Alt Text"
  (support.microsoft.com/en-us/topic/everything-you-need-to-know-to-write-effective
  -alt-text-df98f884-ca3d-456c-807b-1a1fa82f5dc2)

"Federal Social Media Accessibility Toolkit Hackpad"
  (digital.gov/resources/federal-social-media-accessibility-toolkit-hackpad)

"How to Create Accessible Posts on Instagram"
  (www.business2community.com/instagram/how-to-create-accessible-posts-on
  -instagram-02405647)

"Is Your Social Media Accessible to Everyone? These 9 Best Practices Can Help"
  (www.shondaland.com/act/a26294966/make-your-social-media-more-accessible)

"Making Web Images Accessible to People Who Are Blind"
  (consciousstyleguide.com/making-web-images-accessible-people-blind)

"Social Media Accessibility: Inclusive Design Tips for 2024"
  (blog.hootsuite.com/inclusive-design-social-media)

"Start with the 7 Core Skills | Accessible U"
  (accessibility.umn.edu/what-you-can-do/start-7-core-skills)

"Web Accessibility: What, How, and Why"
  (https://www.rabbitwitharedpen.com/blog/web-accessibility-what-how-and-why)

MASTERMIND GROUPS

"5 Essential Rules for Building a Mastermind Group That Gets Results"
  (https://www.score.org/resource/
  blog-post/5-essential-rules-building-a-mastermind-group-gets-results)

"The Power of Mastermind Groups and How You Can Benefit from Them"
  (medium.com/the-post-grad-survival-guide/the-power-of-mastermind-groups-and
  -how-you-can-benefit-from-them-bf4e6eeb66e6)

GOAL SETTING AND PRODUCTIVITY

The Business of Being a Writer by Jane Friedman

Creating the Work You Love: Courage, Commitment, and Career by Rick Jarow

The Daily Stoic: 366 Meditations on Wisdom, Perseverance, and the Art of Living by Ryan
  Holiday & Stephen Hanselman

Deep Work: Rules for Focused Success in a Distracted World by Cal Newport

Four Thousand Weeks: Time Management for Mortals by Oliver Burkeman

"Goal-Setting Strategies"
   (https://medium.com/swlh/goal-setting-strategies-11d8c2c8159b)

"Goal Setting: A Scientific Guide to Setting and Achieving Goals"
   (https://jamesclear.com/goal-setting)

Juggling on a High Wire: The Art of Work-Life Balance When You're Self-Employed by
   Laura Poole

*Just Work: How to Root Out Bias, Prejudice, and Bullying to Build a Kick-Ass Culture of
   Inclusivity* by Kim Scott

*Let My People Go Surfing: The Education of a Reluctant Businessman (Including 10 More Years
   of Business Unusual)* by Yvon Chouinard, founder of Patagonia

Making a Literary Life by Carolyn See

Perfect Bound: How to Navigate the Book Publishing Process Like a Pro by Katherine Pickett

Psycho-Cybernetics: Updated and Expanded by Maxwell Maltz

Slow Productivity: The Lost Art of Accomplishment Without Burnout by Cal Newport

ABOUT THE AUTHOR

Linda Ruggeri is a bilingual freelance nonfiction editor, writer, and creative entrepreneur with a degree in communications and fine arts from Loyola Marymount University. Born to immigrant parents in Los Angeles, Linda is Latina and a first-generation American. Linda is the former Welcome Program director for the EFA, and co-founder alongside Brittany Dowdle of The Networking Studio. Besides being a writer and editor, Linda is an avid urban gardener and baker, and a mom, and would gladly trade any night out for a good nonfiction book and a fine glass of bourbon in her treehouse.

If you liked this book, or found it helpful, the best compliment you can give is leaving your honest review at the store where you bought this book, or to post about it on social media, so that other writers who want to create a better community and better contacts can find it. This book is just one of the offerings we have at The Networking Studio, so do check out our website, www.thenetworkingstudio.com, to see what other treats you can find there.